Michael Drayton

The Barons' Wars, Nymphidia, and other Poems

Michael Drayton

The Barons' Wars, Nymphidia, and other Poems

ISBN/EAN: 9783744710336

Printed in Europe, USA, Canada, Australia, Japan

Cover: Foto ©Thomas Meinert / pixelio.de

More available books at **www.hansebooks.com**

THE BARONS' WARS

NYMPHIDIA

AND OTHER POEMS

BY

MICHAEL DRAYTON

WITH AN INTRODUCTION BY HENRY MORLEY
LL.D., PROFESSOR OF ENGLISH LITERATURE AT
UNIVERSITY COLLEGE, LONDON

LONDON
GEORGE ROUTLEDGE AND SONS
BROADWAY, LUDGATE HILL
GLASGOW AND NEW YORK
1887

INTRODUCTION.

MICHAEL DRAYTON was only a year older than his friend Shakespeare, and born in the same county. As Thomas Fuller says, when writing of him among Warwickshire Worthies, "Michael Drayton was born within a few miles of William Shakespeare, his countryman and fellow-poet, and buried within fewer paces of Geoffrey Chaucer and Edward Spenser." Drayton's birth year was 1563, his birth-place Hartshill, halfway between Atherstone and Nuneaton, near the north-eastern border of Warwickshire. Close by, in Leicestershire, just over the border, is that one of the many English parishes called Drayton—Fenny Drayton—from which his family may have derived its name. The river Anker flows by pleasant hills and woods, where there was once the Forest of Arden; it flows near to Hartshill on its way to join the Tame at Tamworth, and they were its waters that fed the Drayton fens. The Anker is the home river whose ripples are heard also in Drayton's song:

"Fair Arden, thou my Tempé art alone,
And thou, sweet Anker, art my Helicon."

Drayton's Anker thus became associated with a poet's life, like Herrick's Dean Burn, or Spenser's Mulla. When celebrating Warwickshire, the middle shire of England, in his "Polyolbion"—"that shire which we the heart of England well may call"—Drayton speaks of it as his native county—

"My native country then, which so brave spirits hast bred,
If there be virtue yet remaining in thy earth,
Or any good of thine thou breath'dst into my birth,
Accept it as thine own whilst now I sing of thee;
Of all thy later brood th' unworthiest though I be."

Drayton found patrons in his boyhood and youth. His earliest helper was a Warwickshire man, Sir Henry Goodyere of Polesworth, about seven miles northward of Hartshill, who is said to have maintained him for some time at Oxford, and by whom he was introduced to the Countess of Bedford. Sir Walter Aston also gave substantial help to Drayton in his early life; but of that early life little is known.

It was at the age of eight-and-twenty that Michael Drayton published his first volume of verse. That first book, dedicated to Lady Jane Devereux of Merivale, was described in its title as "The Harmonie of the Church, containing the Spiritual Songs and Holy Hymns of Godly Men, Patriarchs and Prophets, all sweetly sounding to the Glory of the Highest, now (newly) reduced into sundry kinds of English metre: meet to be read or sung, for the solace and comfort of the godly." John Whitgift was then Archbishop of Canterbury, suppressing epigrams and other writings of the poets, and it pleased him to order the destruction of Drayton's volumes, except forty copies which he seized and kept. The Archbishop, who was "bridling the Puritans," perhaps suspected Puritanism in a book professing to be "for the solace and comfort of the godly."

In 1593 Drayton published love sonnets and pastorals under the title of "Idea"; "The Shepherd's Garland," fashioned in nine eclogues; "Rowland's Sacrifice to the Nine Muses," taking Rowland for his own pastoral name; and in 1594 these were followed by "Idea's Mirror," "Amours in Quatorzains," and his "Matilda," written in Chaucer's stanza. There is a robust freshness in Drayton's love poems that suggests an independent spirit in their writer. They were addressed to the lady of whose late coming to town Drayton playfully complained in one of his Elegies, and of whom he said in a sonnet to his native river—

"Arden's sweet Anker, let thy glory be
That fair Idea only lives by thee;"

but there may have been no more in them than, according to poetic form, a poet's playful celebration of her graces. Drayton lived to the age of sixty-eight, and died a bachelor.

From strains of love that earned him credit among wits and scholars of Elizabeth's Court, Drayton passed to strains of war in the latter years of the reign, when there was no direct heir to the throne, and none knew that Elizabeth—who, for her own politic reasons, had not named a successor—had agreed privately with her council upon all steps to be taken to make the succession sure. It suited her well that a politic omission should be set down to her petticoat. But among her subjects there was widespread expectation that the Queen's death would be made the signal for another civil war. Lodge for that reason wrote his play on Marius and Sylla, called "The Wounds of Civil War." The Second and Third of the Three Parts of Henry VI. on which Shakespeare worked, had the same thought in them. And the poets who wrote during Elizabeth's last years the two chief heroic poems of their time took for their warning themes the two great Civil Wars of the past; Michael Drayton, the Barons' Wars, and Samuel Daniel the wars of York and Lancaster.

Drayton's poem first appeared in 1596 as "Mortimeriados; the Lamentable Civil Wars of Edward the Second and the Barons." He had begun to write this poem in Chaucer's seven-lined stanza, but finding that too sweet for a tale of discord and war, rewrote the opening, and completed the work in the Italian octave rhyme, which the strong influence of Italy upon our literature had brought into new prominence, and which was used by Daniel also for his poem upon civil war.

In the same year (1596) Drayton produced his "Legend of Robert Duke of Normandy;" and in 1597 he produced, in imitation of Ovid's "Heroides," "England's Heroical Epistles." He then worked afresh upon his "Mortimeriados," which was enlarged and published in 1603, under the title it now bears, "The Barons' Wars."

In the same year (1603) Drayton welcomed the new reign with a Gratulatory Poem, "To the Majestie of King James," which was ungraciously received. He turned with contempt from the cloud of James's new knights, and the meaner life that gathered about the meaner Court of the new sovereign. James, though a Solomon in his own eyes, and warranted a Solomon by Francis Bacon, had mean tastes, and low-minded men stood high in his favour. Daniel as well as Drayton complained bitterly of change of times. Daniel turned his back upon the Court and town, and went away to turn farmer at Beckington. Drayton turned from the Court, and what he thought of it will be found here in some of his Elegies; but he gave himself with new devotion to his Muse. In 1604 he published a satire, "The Owl." In 1605 he published an edition of his "Barons' Wars," with his historical poems, and "Idea." Then he set to work manfully on the long labour of a poetical description of his native land, which he called "Polyolbion" (Many-ways-Happy), of which eighteen books, in Alexandrine verse, were published in 1613; twelve more books followed in 1622; all being illustrated with maps of the several counties described, and notes by his friend John Selden.

In 1627 Drayton published a volume containing pieces written in the reign of James. "The Battle of Agincourt" stood first in it, and was followed by some of his daintiest work. It included the delightful fairy mock heroic of the wrath and madness of Oberon, his "Nymphidia," with his "Elegies," and some strains of sweet music in which the poet poured out his affection for his Muse. As we pass from the Elegies in which the poet paints the evil times, we read easily between the lines of his enthusiasm in "The Quest of Cynthia," a song of the search for ideal beauty alike in motive to Keats's "Endymion." We may understand also the peril of the Shepherd's Sirena to whom her lover can go over only by giving his own life to save hers.

"Could I give what thou dost crave,
To that pass thy state is grown,
I thereby thy life may save,
But am sure to lose mine own."

We may understand why his fellow-shepherds, fellow-poets, warn him to be up and doing.

"For our fields 'tis time to stand,
Or they quickly will be gone,
Roguish swineherds, that repine
At our flocks like beastly clowns,
Swear that they will bring their swine,
And will root up all our downs."

We cannot afford to drop out of companionship a poet so full as Drayton is of grace and vigour. His way of life was very quiet; he loved his friends, and counted among them some of the chief poets and best thinkers of his time. Thomas Fuller, who was twenty-three years old when Drayton died, records of him "that he was a pious poet, his conscience having always the command of his fancy, very temperate in his life, slow of speech, and inoffensive in company. He changed his laurel for a crown of glory, Anno 1631." His piety was that which does not vaunt itself, and gives the sound foundation for a hearty cheerfulness; his quiet in society was that of a mind accustomed to wait and think.

H. M.

February 1887.

THE BARONS' WARS,

IN THE REIGN OF EDWARD THE SECOND.

THE FIRST CANTO.

THE ARGUMENT.

<blockquote>
The grievous plagues, and the prodigious signs,
That this great war and slaughter do foreshow ;
The cause which the proud Baronage combines,
The Queen's much wrong, whence many mischiefs grow ;
And how the time to this great change inclines,
As with what arms each country men do go,
   What cause to yield the Mortimers pretend,
   And their commitment doth this Canto end.
</blockquote>

I.

THE bloody factions and rebellious pride
Of a strong nation, whose ill-managed might
The Prince and Peers did many a day divide ;
With whom wrong was no wrong, nor right no right,
Whose strife their swords knew only to decide,
Spurred to their high speed by their equal spite,
   Me from soft lays and tender loves doth bring,
   Of a far worse than civil war to sing,

2.

What hellish fury poisoned their hot blood?
Or can we think 'twas in the power of charms,
With those so poor hopes of the public good,
To have enticed them to tumultuous arms,
And from that safety, wherein late they stood,
Wrest them so far from feeling of their harms,
 That France and Belgia with affrighted eyes
 Stood both amazed at their miseries?

3.

The inveterate malice in their bosoms bred
Who for their Charter waged a former war,
Their angry sires, in them that venom fed,
As their true heirs of many a wide-mouthed scar:
Or was't the blood they had in conquest shed,
Having enlarged their country's bounds so far,
 That did themselves against themselves oppose,
 With blades of Bilbo changing English blows?

4.

O Thou, the wise director of my muse,
Upon whose bounty all my powers depend,
Into my breast thy sacredst fire infuse;
Ravish my spirit this great work to attend:
Let the still night my laboured lines peruse,
That when my poems gain their wishéd end,
 Such whose sad eyes shall read this tragic story,
 In my weak hand may see thy might and glory.

5.

What care would plot, dissension strove to cross,
Which like an earthquake rent the tottering State ;
In war abroad they suffered public loss,
And were at home despoiled by private hate :
Whilst them those strange calamities did toss
(For there was none that nourished not debate),
　　Confusion did the common peace confound,
　　No help at hand, yet mortal was their wound.

6.

Thou Church, then swelling in thy mightiness,
Which in thy hand so ample power didst hold
To stay those factions ere their full excess,
Which at thy pleasure thou might'st have controlled,
Why didst not thou those outrages suppress,
Which to all times thy praise might have enrolled ?
　　Thou shouldst to them have laid thy Holy Word,
　　And not thy hand to the unholy sword.

7.

Bloodthirsty war arising first from hell,
And seizing on this chief part of the isle,
Where it before near forty years did dwell,
And with abhorred pollution did defile,
In which so many a famous soldier fell ;
By Edward Longshanks banishéd awhile,
　　Transferred to Wales and to Albania, there
　　To ruin them as it had ravined here.

8.

Where hovering long with inauspicious wings
About the verge of these distempered climes,
By coming back new mischief hither brings,
To work them up to those disastrous crimes;
Weakeneth their power by her diminishings:
And taking fast hold on those wicked times,
   So far enforced their fury, that at length
   It cracked the nerves which knit their ancient strength.

9.

Whose frightful vision, at the first approach,
With violent madness struck that desperate age;
And did not only those rebellions broach
Amongst the commons, but the devilish rage
Did on the best nobility encroach,
And in their damned conspiracies engage
   The royal blood, them likewise down to bring
   By unnatural treasons to their natural King.

10.

When in the North (whilst horror yet was young)
Those dangerous seasons swiftly coming on,
Whilst o'er their heads portentous meteors hung,
And in the skies stern comets brightly shone,
Prodigious births were intermixed among,
Such as before to times had been unknown:
   In bloody issues forth the earth doth break,
   Weeping for them whose woes it could not speak.

11.

And by the rankness of contagious air
A mortal plague invadeth man and beast,
Which far dispersed, and raging everywhere,
In doubt the same too quickly should have ceased
To assure them of the slaughter being near,
Yet was by famine cruelly increased ;
    As though the heavens in their remissful doom
    Took those they loved from worser days to come.

12.

The level course that we intend to go
Now to the end, that ye may clearly see,
And that we every circumstance may show,
The state of things, and truly what they be,
And our materials how we do bestow,
With each occurrent right in his degree ;
    From these portents we now divert our view,
    To bring to pass the horrors that ensue.

13.

The calling back of banished Gaveston,
'Gainst which the Barons had to Longshanks sworn ;
The seigniories and high promotion,
Him in his lawless courses to suborn ;
The abetting of that wanton minion,
Who held the old nobility in scorn ;
    Stirred up that hateful and outrageous strife
    Which cost so many an Englishman his life.

14.

O much loved Lacy, hadst thou spared that breath,
Which shortly after Nature thee denied,
To Lancaster delivered at thy death,
To whom thy only daughter was affied,
Taking for pledge his knightly oath and faith,
Stiffly to stick upon the Barons' side ;
   Thy manors, rents, and titles of renown
   Had not so soon been forfeit to the Crown.

15.

Those lordships Bruse to those two Spensers past,
Crossing the Barons' vehement desire ;
As from Jove's arm that fearful lightning cast,
That fifty towns lay spent in hostile fire :
Alas, too vain and prodigal a waste,
The strong effect of their conceivéd ire,
   Urging the weak King by a violent hand
   To abjure those false lords from the troubled land.

16.

When as the fair Queen progressing in Kent,
Was there denied her entrance into Leeds
By Badlesmer, a Baron eminent.
Against the King, that in this course proceeds,
Which further addeth to their discontent
A special spring, which this great mischief feeds :
   Wrong upon wrong, by heaping more and more,
   To thrust on that which went too fast before.

17.

Which more and more King Edward's hate
    increased,
Whose mind ran still on Gaveston degraded,
The thoughts of which so settled in his breast
That it had all his faculties invaded,
Which for the Spensers happened out the best,
By whom thereto he chiefly was persuaded ;
    And by whose counsels he ere long was led
    To leave his bright Queen, and to fly her bed.

18.

That she herself who, whilst she stood in grace,
Employed her powers these discords to appease
When yet confusion had not fully place,
In times not grown so dangerous as these,
A party made in their afflicted case,
Her willing hand to his destruction lays ;
    That time, whose soft palm heals the wound of war,
    May cure the sore, but never close the scar.

19.

In all that heat, then gloriously began
The serious subject of my solid vein,
Brave Mortimer, that somewhat more than man,
Of the old heroes' great and godlike strain,
For whom invention doing all it can,
His weight of honour hardly shall sustain,
    To bear his name immortalized, and high,
    When he in earth unnumbered years shall lie.

20.

Whose uncle then, whose name his nephew bare,
The only comfort of the woful Queen,
Who from his cradle held him as his care,
In whom so many early hopes were seen,
For this young lord most wisely doth prepare,
Whilst yet her deep heart-goring wound was green,
   And on this fair advantage firmly wrought
   To place him highly in her princely thought.

21.

This was the man at whose unusual birth
The stars were said to counsel to retire,
And in aspects of happiness and mirth
Marked him a spirit to greatness to aspire,
That had no mixture of the drossy earth,
But all compact of perfect heavenly fire;
   So well made up, that such a one as he,
   Jove in a man like Mortimer would be.

22.

The quickening virtue of which nobler part
With so rare pureness rectified his blood,
And to so high a temper wrought his heart,
That it could not be locked within a flood,
That no misfortune possibly could thwart;
Which from the native greatness where it stood,
   Showed, at the first, the pitch it was to fly
   Could not with less be bounded than the sky.

23.

Worthy the grandchild of so great a lord,
Who, whilst our Longshanks fortunately reigned,
Re-edified King Arthur's ancient board,
Which he at goodly Kenilworth ordained,
And to that former glory it restored,
To which a hundred gallant knights retained
   With all the pomp that might become a Court
   Or might give honour to that martial sport.

24.

The heart-swoln lords with fury throughly fired,
Whom Edward's wrongs to vengeance still provoke,
With Lancaster and Hertford had conspired,
No more to bear the Spensers' servile yoke:
The time is come that they a change desired,
That they (the bonds of their allegiance broke)
   Resolved with blood their liberty to buy,
   And in the quarrel vowed to live and die.

25.

What privilege hath our free birth, they say,
Or in our blood what virtue doth remain?
To each lascivious minion made a prey,
That us and our nobility disdain
Whilst they in triumph boast of our decay;
Either those spirits we never did retain
   That were our fathers', or by fate we fall
   Both from their greatness, liberty, and all.

26.

Our honour lifted from that sovereign state
From whence at first it challengéd the being,
And prostitute to infamy and hate,
As with itself in all things disagreeing;
Quite out of order, disproportionate,
From the right way preposterously flying:
    Whilst others are themselves, and only we
    Are not held those we would but seem to be.

27.

Then to what end hath our great conquest served,
Those acts achievéd by the Norman sword,
Our charters, patents, and our deeds reserved
Our offices and titles to record,
The crests that on our monuments are carved,
If they to us no greater good afford?
    Thus do they murmur every one apart,
    With many a vexed soul, many a grieved heart.

28.

This while the Queen into deep sorrow thrown,
Wherein she wastes her goodly youth away,
Beyond belief, to all but Heaven unknown,
This spark till now that closely covered lay,
By the sharp breath of desp'rate faction blown,
Converts her long night to a wishéd day,
    Her woful winter of misfortune cheering,
    As the dark world at the bright sun's appearing.

29.

Though much perplexed amidst these hard
extremes,
Whilst helps fall short that should her hopes prefer,
Nor clearly yet could she discern those beams
To her desires that else might lighten her,
Her thoughts oft changing, like deceitful dreams,
In her sad breast such violent passions stir
   That (striving which each other should control)
   Work strange confusion in her troubled soul.

30.

To be debarred of that imperial state
Which to her graces rightly did belong,
Basely rejected, and repudiate,
A virtuous lady, goodly, fair, and young;
These with such fervour still do intimate
Her too much settled and inveterate wrong,
   That to the least all pardon she denies,
   With arguments of her indignities.

31.

Whilst to despatch the angry heavens pursue
What there unjudged had many a day depended,
When all these mischiefs to full ripeness grew,
And in their harvest hasting to be ended:
For all these lines into one centre drew,
Which way soe'er they seemed to be extended,
   And all together in proportion laid,
   Although but small, add somewhat to her aid.

32.

Now comes the time when Mortimer doth enter,
Of great employment in this tragic act,
His youth and courage boldly bid him venter,
Prompting him still how strongly he was backed;
Who at this time, even as from Heaven was sent her,
When the straight course to her desire was tracked,
    And she upon more certainty doth stay,
    In a direct, although a dangerous way.

33.

This dreadful comet drew her wond'ring eye,
Which soon began his golden head to rear,
Whose glorious fixure in so clear a sky,
Struck the beholder with a horrid fear;
And in a region elevate so high,
And by the form wherein it did appear,
    As the most skilful wisely did divine,
    Foreshowed the kingdom shortly to decline.

34.

Yet still recoiling at the Spensers' power,
So often checked with their intemperate pride,
The inconstant Barons wavering every hour
The fierce encounter of this boist'rous tide
That easily might her livelihood devour,
Had she not those that skilfully could guide,
    She from suspicion cunningly retires,
    Careless in show of what she most desires.

35.

Dissembling so, as one that knew not ill,
So can she rule the greatness of her mind,
As a most perfect rect'ress of her will,
Above the usual weakness of her kind,
For all these storms, immovable and still,
Her secret drift the wisest miss to find ;
   Nor will she know yet what these factions meant,
   But with a pleaséd eye soothes sad discontent.

36.

The least suspicion craftily to heal,
Still in her looks humility she bears,
The safest way with mightiness to deal,
So Policy Religion's habit wears;
'Twas then no time her grievance to reveal,
" He's mad who takes a lion by the ears."
   This knew the Queen, and this well know the wise,
   This must they learn that rightly temporize.

37.

The bishop Torleton, learnedst of the land
Upon a text of politics to preach,
Which he long studying well did understand
And by a method could as aptly teach ;
He was a prelate of a potent hand,
Wise was the man that went beyond his reach :
   This subtle tutor Isabel had taught
   Points, into which King Edward never sought.

38.

Rage, which no longer limits can contain,
Lastly breaks forth into a public flame,
Their slipped occasion better to regain
When to their purpose things so fitly frame,
And now discernéd visibly and plain
When treason boldly dare its right proclaim,
   Casting aside all secular disguise,
   Doth with proud legions furiously arise

39.

As Severn lately in her ebbs that sank,
Vast and forsaken, leaves the uncovered sands,
Fetching full tides, luxurious, high, and rank,
Seems in her pride to invade the neighb'ring lands,
Breaking her limits, covering all her banks,
Threateneth the proud hills with her watery hands;
   As though she meant her empiry to have,
   Where even but lately she beheld her grave.

40.

Through all the land, from places far and near,
Led to the field as fortune lots their side,
With the ancient weapons used in war to bear,
As those directed when they chose their guide;
Or else perhaps as they affected were,
Or as by friendship or by duty tied;
   Swayed by the strength and motion of their blood,
   No cause examined, be it bad or good.

41.

From Norfolk, and the countries of the east,
That with the pike most skilfully could fight;
Then those of Kent, unconquered of the rest,
That to this day maintain their ancient right;
For courage no whit second to the best,
The Cornish men most active, bold, and light;
 Those near the plain, the pole-axe best that wield,
 And claim for theirs the vaward of the field.

42.

The noble Welsh of the ancient British race;
From Lancashire men famous for their bows;
The men of Cheshire chiefest for their place,
Of bone so big, as only made for blows,
Which for their faith are had in special grace,
And have been ever fearful to their foes;
 The Northern then, in feuds so deadly fell,
 That for their spear and horsemanship excel.

43.

All that for use experience could espy:
Such as in fens and marsh-lands use to trade,
The doubtful fords and passages to try
With stilts and lope-staves that do aptliest wade,
Most fit for scouts and currers, to descry;
Those from the mines with pickaxe and with spade
 For pioneers best, that for intrenching are
 Men chiefly needful in the use of war.

44.

O noble nation, furnishéd with arms,
So full of spirit, as almost matched by none!
Had Heaven but blest thee to foresee thy harms,
And as thy valiant nephews did, have gone
Paris, Rouen, Orleans, shaking with alarms,
As the bright sun thy glory then had shone:
　To other realms thou hadst transferred this chance,
　Nor had your sons been first that conquered France.

45.

And thus on all hands setting up their rest,
And all make forward for this mighty day,
Where every one prepares to do his best,
When at the stake their lives and fortunes lay,
No cross event their purposes to wrest,
Being now on in so direct a way:
　Yet whilst they play this strange and doubtful game,
　The Queen stands off, and secretly gives aim.

46.

But Mortimer his foot had scarcely set
Into the road where fortune had to deal,
But she, disposed his forward course to let,
Her lewd condition quickly doth reveal,
Glory to her vain deity to get
By him, whose strange birth bears her ominous seal,
　Taking occasion from that very hour,
　In him to prove and manifest her power.

47.

As when we see the early rising sun,
With his bright beams to emulate our sight;
But when his course yet newly is begun,
The hum'rous fogs deprive us of his light,
Till through the clouds he his clear forehead run,
Climbing the noontide in his glorious height:
  His clear beginning Fortune cloudeth thus,
  To make his midday great and glorious,

48.

The King, discreetly, that considered,
The space of earth whereon the Barons stand
As what the powers to them contributed,
Then being himself but partner of his land;
Of the small strength and army that he led
'Gainst them which did so great a power command,
  Wisely about him doth begin to look:
  Great was the task which now he undertook.

49.

And warned by danger to misdoubt the worst,
In equal scales whilst either's fortunes hung,
He must perform the utmost that he durst,
Or undergo intolerable wrong:
As good to stir, as after be enforced;
To stop the source whence all these mischiefs sprung,
  He with the marchers thinks best to begin,
  Which first must lose, ere he could hope to

50.

The Mortimers being men of greatest might,
Whose name was dreadful and commanded far,
Sturdy to manage, of a haughty spright,
Strongly allied, much followed, popular,
On whom if he but happily could light,
He hoped more easily to conclude the war :
  Which he intendeth speedily to try,
  To quit that first which most stood in his eye.

51.

For which he expeditiously provided
That part of land into his power to get
Which, if made good, might keep his foes divided;
Their combination cunningly to let,
Which, should they join, would be so strongly sided,
Two mighty hosts, together safely met,
  The face of war would look so stern and great,
  As it might threat to heave him from his seat.

52.

Wherefore the King from London setteth forth
With a full army, furnished of the best,
Accompanied with men of special worth,
Which to this war his promises had prest.
Great Lancaster was lord of all the North,
The Mortimers were masters of the West,
  He towards mid-England makes the way 'twixt
    either,
  Which they must cross ere they could come to-
    gether.

53.

Strongly inveigled with delightful hope,
Stoutly to affront and shoulder with debate,
Knowing to meet with a resolvéd troop
That came prepared with courage and with hate,
Whose stubborn crests if he enforced to stoop
It him behoves to tempt some powerful fate,
   And through stern guards of swords and hostile fire
   Make way to peace, or shamefully retire.

54.

When now the marchers well upon their way
(Expecting those that them supplies should bring,
Which had too long abused them by delay)
Were suddenly encountered by the King ;
They then perceive that dilatory stay
To be the causer of their ruining,
   When at their bosoms black destruction stood,
   With open jaws preparéd for their blood.

55.

And by the shifting of the inconstant wind,
Seeing what weather they were like to meet,
Which even at first so awkwardly they find
Before they could give sea-room to their fleet,
Clean from their course and cast so far behind,
And yet in peril every hour to split,
   Some unknown harbour suddenly must sound,
   Or run their fortunes desperately on ground.

56.

The elder Peer, grave, politic, and wise,
Which had all dangers absolutely scanned,
Finding high time his nephew to advise,—
Since now their state stood on this desperate hand,
And from this mischief many more to rise,
Which his experience made him understand,—
"Nephew (saith he) 'tis but in vain to strive,
 Counsel must help our safety to contrive.

57.

"The downright peril present in our eye,
Not to be shunned, we see what it assures;
Think then what weight upon our fall doth lie,
And what our being this design procures,
As, to our friends what good may grow thereby;
Prove, which the test of reason best endures:
 For who observes strict policy's true laws,
 Shifts his proceeding to the varying cause.

58.

"To hazard fight with the imperial powers,
Will our small troops undoubtedly appal;
Then this our war us wilfully devours,
Yielding ourselves, yet thus we lose not all,
We leave our friends this smaller force of ours,
Reserved for them, though haplessly we fall:
 That weakness ever hath a glorious hand,
 That falls itself to make the cause to stand.

59.

" 'Twixt unexpected and so dangerous ills
That's saf'st, wherein we smallest peril see,
Which to make choice of, reason justly wills,
And it doth best with policy agree :
The idle vulgar breath it nothing skills,
'Tis sound discretion must our pilot be ;
   He that doth still the fairest means prefer,
   Answers opinion howsoe'er he err.

60.

" And to the world's eye seeming yet so strong,
By our descending willingly from hence,
'Twill show we were provokéd by our wrong,
Not having other sinister pretence :
This force left off that doth to us belong,
Will in opinion lessen our offence :
   Men are not ever incident to loss,
   When fortune seems them frowardly to cross.

61.

" Nor give we envy absolute excess,
To search so far our subtleties to find,
There's nearer means this mischief to redress,
And make successful what is yet behind ;
Let's not ourselves of all hope dispossess,
Fortune is ever variously inclined :
   A small advantage in the affairs of Kings,
   Guides a slight means to compass mighty
     things."

62.

This speech so caught his nephew's pliant youth
(Who his grave Eme did ever much respect)
Proceeding from integrity and truth :
Well could he counsel, well could he direct
With strong persuasions, which he still pursu'th,
Which in a short time showed by the effect,
 A wise man's counsel by a secret fate,
 Seeming from reason, yet proves fortunate.

63.

To which the King they gravely do invite,
By the most strict and ceremonious way ;
No circumstance omitted, nor no rite
That might give colour to their new essay,
Or that applause might publicly excite,
To which the King doth willingly obey :
 Who like themselves, in feeling danger near,
 Rather accepts a doubt than certain fear.

64.

Which he receives in presage of his good,
To his success auspiciously applied,
Which somewhat cooled his much distempered blood,
Ere he their force in doubtful arms had tried ;
And whilst they thus in his protection stood,
At his disposing wholly to abide,
 He first in safety doth dismiss their power,
 Then sends them both his prisoners to the Tower.

65.

O all-preparing Providence divine,
In thy large book what secrets are enrolled!
What sundry helps doth thy great power assign,
To prop the course which thou intend'st to hold!
What mortal sense is able to define
Thy mysteries, thy counsels manifold?
   It is thy Wisdom strangely that extends
   Obscure proceedings to apparent ends.

66.

This was the means by which the Fates dispose
More dreadful plagues upon that age, to bring
Utter confusion on the heads of those
That were before the Barons' ruining;
With the subversion of the public's foes,
The murder of the miserable King;
   And that which 'came castrophe to all,
   Great Mortimer's inevitable fall.

67.

This to these troubles lends a little breath,
As the first pause to hearten this affair,
And for a while defers oft-threatening death,
Whilst each their breach by leisure would repair,
And as a bound their fury limiteth.
But in this manner whilst things strangely fare,
   Horror beyond all wonted bounds doth swell,
   As the next Canto fearfully shall tell.

THE SECOND CANTO.

THE ARGUMENT.

At Burton Bridge the puissant powers are met;
The form and order of the doubtful fight,
Whereas the King the victory doth get,
And the proud Barons are enforced to flight;
When they again towards Borough forward set,
Where they by him were vanquishéd outright:
　Lastly, the laws do execute their power
　On those which there the sword did not devour.

1.

THIS chance of war, that suddenly had swept
So large a share from their selected store,
Which for their help they carefully had kept,
That to their aid might still have added more,
By this ill luck into their army crept,
Made them much weaker than they were before:
　So that the Barons reinforced their bands,
　Finding their hearts to stand in need of hands.

2.

For deadly hate so long and deeply rooted,
Could not abide to hear the name of peace,
So that discretion but a little booted
'Gainst that, thereby which only did increase:
For the least grief by malice was promoted,
Anger set on, beginning to surcease;
　So that all counsel much their ears offended
　But what to spoil and sad invasion tended.

3.

All up in action for the public cause,
Scarcely the mean'st but he a party stood,
Taxed by the letter of the censuring laws
In his estate, if failing in his blood ;
And who was freest, entangled by some clause ;
Which to their fury gives continual food,
    For where confusion once hath gotten hold,
    Till all fall flat, it hardly is controlled.

4.

And now by night, whenas pale leaden sleep
Upon their eyelids heavily did dwell
And step by step on every sense did creep,
Mischief, that black inhabitant of hell,
Which never fails continual watch to keep,
Fearful to think, a horrid thing to tell,
    Entered the place whereas those warlike lords
    Lay mailed in armour, girt with ireful swords.

5.

She, with a sharp sight and a meagre look,
Was always prying where she might do ill,
In which the fiend continual pleasure took
(Her starvéd body plenty could not fill),
Searching in every corner, every nook,
With wingéd feet, too swift to work her will,
    Furnished with deadly instruments she went
    Of every sort, to wound whereso she meant.

6.

Having a vial filled with baneful wrath
(Brought from Cocytus by that cursed spright),
Which in her pale hand purposely she hath,
And drops the poison upon every wight ;
For to each one she knew the ready path,
Though in the midst and dead time of the night ;
    Whose strength too soon invadeth every Peer,
    Not one escaped her that she cometh near.

7.

That the next morning breaking in the east,
With a much troubled and affrighted mind,
Each whom this venom lately did infest,
The strong effect in their swoln stomachs find;
Now doth the poison boil in every breast,
To sad destruction every one's inclined ;
    Rumours of spoil through every ear doth fly,
    And threatening fury sits in every eye.

8.

This done, in haste she to King Edward hies,
Who late grown proud upon his good success,
His time to feasts and wantonness applies,
And with crowned cups his sorrows doth suppress,
Upon his fortune wholly that relies,
And in the bosom of his courtly press,
    Vaunteth the hap of this victorious day,
    Whilst the sick land in sorrow pines away.

9.

Thither she comes, and in a minion's shape
She getteth near the person of the King ;
And as he tastes the liquor of the grape,
Into the cup her poison she doth wring :
Not the least drop untainted doth escape,
For to that purpose she her store did bring :
　Whose strong commixture, as the sequel tried,
　Filled his hot veins with arrogance and pride.

10.

That having both such courage and such might
As to so great a business did belong,
Neither yet think by their unnatural fight
What the Republic suffered them among :
For misty error so deludes their sight
(Which still betwixt them and clear reason hung),
　And their opinions in such sort abused,
　As that their fault can never be excused.

11.

Now our Minerva puts on dreadful arms
Further to wade into this bloody war,
And from her slumber wakened with alarms
Riseth to sing of many a massacre,
Of gloomy magics and benumbing charms,
Of many a deep wound, many a fearful scar :
　For that low sock wherein she used to tread,
　Marching in greaves, a helmet on her head.

12.

Whilst thus vain hope doth these false lords
 delude,
Who having drawn their forces to a head,
They their full purpose seriously pursued,
By Lancaster and valiant Hertford led,
Their long proceeding lastly to conclude ;
Whilst now to meet both armies hotly sped,
    The Barons taking Burton in their way,
    Till they could hear where Edward's army lay.

13.

To which report too suddenly bewrayed
Their manner of encamping, and the place,
Their present strength, and their expected aid,
As what might most avail them in this case.
The speedy march the imperial power had made,
Had brought them soon within a little space :
    For still the King conducted had his force
    Which way he heard the Barons bent their course.

14.

Upon the east, from bushy Needwood's side,
There riseth up an easy climbing hill,
At whose fair foot the silver Trent doth slide
And the slow air with her soft murmuring fill,
Which with the store of liberal brooks supplied
The insatiate meads continually doth swill,
    Over whose stream a bridge of wondrous strength
    Leads on from Burton, to that hill in length.

15.

Upon the mount the King his tentage fixed,
And in the town the Barons lay in sight,
Whenas the Trent was risen so betwixt,
That for a while prolonged the unnatural fight
With many waters that itself had mixed,
To stay their fury doing all it might :
    Things which presage both good and ill there be,
    Which Heaven foreshows, but will not let us see.

16.

The Heaven even mourning o'er our heads doth sit,
Grieving to see the times so out of course,
Looking on them who never look at it,
And in mere pity melteth with remorse,
Longer from tears that could not stay a whit,
Whose influence on every lower source,
    From the swoln fluxure of the clouds, doth shake
    A rank imposthume upon every lake.

17.

O warlike nation, hold thy conquering hand,
Even senseless things do warn thee yet to pause ;
Thy mother soil, on whom thou armed dost stand,
Which should restrain thee by all natural laws,
Canst thou, unkind, inviolate that band ?
Nay, heaven and earth are angry with the cause :
    Yet stay thy foot in mischief's ugly gate,
    Ill comes too soon, repentance oft too late.

18.

O, can the clouds weep over thy decay,
Yet not one drop fall from thy droughty eyes?
Seest thou the snare, and wilt not shun the way,
Nor yet be warned by passéd miseries?
'Tis yet but early in this dismal day,
Let late experience learn thee to be wise:
   An ill foreseen may easily be prevented,
   But happed, unhelped, though ne'er enough lamented.

19.

Cannot the Scot of your late slaughter boast?
And are ye yet scarce healéd of the sore?
Is't not enough ye have already lost,
But your own madness must needs make it more?
Will ye seek safety in some foreign coast?
Your wives and children pitied ye before:
   But when your own bloods your own swords embrue,
   Who pities them who should have pitied you?

20.

The neighbouring groves are spoiléd of their trees
For boats and timber to essay the flood,
Where men are labouring as 'twere summer bees,
Some hollowing trunks, some binding heaps of wood,
Some on their breasts, some working on their knees,
To win the bank whereon the Barons stood;
   Which o'er the current they by strength must tew,
   To shed that blood which many an age shall rue.

21.

Some sharp their swords, some right their morions
    set,
Their greaves and pouldrons others rivet fast,
The archers now their bearded arrows whet,
Whilst everywhere the clamorous drums are brassed ;
Some taking view where they sure ground might get,
Not one but some advantage doth forecast :
    With ranks and files each plain and meadow swarms,
    As all the land were clad in angry arms.

22.

The crests and badges of each nobler name
Against their owners rudely seem to stand,
As angry for the achievements whence they came
That to their fathers gave that generous brand.
O ye unworthy of your ancient fame,
Against yourselves to lift your conquering hand,
    Since foreign swords your height could not abate,
    By your own pride yourselves to ruinate!

23.

Upon his surcoat valiant Nevil bore
A silver saltire upon martial red ;
A lady's sleeve high-spirited Hastings wore,
Ferrer his tabard with rich verry spread,
Well known in many a warlike match before ;
A raven set on Corbet's arméd head,
    And Culpepper in silver arms enrailed,
    Bear thereupon a bloody bend engrailed.

24.

The noble Percy in this dreadful day,
With a bright crescent in his guidon came,
In his white cornet Verdon doth display
A fret of gules, prized in this mortal game,
That had been seen in many a doubtful fray,
His lances' pennons stainéd with the same ;
  The angry horse, chafed with the stubborn bit,
  With his hard hoof the earth in fury smit.

25.

I could the sum of Stafford's arming show,
What colours Ross and Courtney did unfold,
Great Warren's blazon I could let you know,
And all the glorious circumstance have told,
Named every ensign as they stood arow ;
But O, dear Muse, too soon thou art controlled !
  For in remembrance of their evil speed,
  My pen, for ink, warm drops of blood doth shed.

26.

On the King's part the imperial standard's pitched,
With all the hatchments of the English crown,
Great Lancaster, with no less power enriched,
Sets the same leopards in his colours down.
O, if ye be not frantic or bewitched,
Yet do but see that on yourselves you frown :
  A little note of difference is in all,
  How can the same stand, when the same doth fall ?

27.

Behold the eagles, lions, talbots, bears,
The badges of your famous ancestries;
Shall those brave marks by their inglorious heirs
Stand thus opposed against their families?
More ancient arms no Christian nation bears,
Relics unworthy of their progenies;
 Those beasts ye bear do in their kinds agree,
 O, that than beasts more savage men should be!

28.

And whilst the King doth in sad council sit,
How he might best the other bank recover,
See how misfortune still her time can fit;
Such as were sent the country to discover
(As up and down from place to place they flit),
Had found a ford to pass their forces over;
 Ill news hath wings, and with the wind doth go,
 Comfort's a cripple, and comes ever slow.

29.

When Edward, fearing Lancaster's supplies,
Proud Richmond, Surrey, and great Pembroke sent,
On whose success he mightily relies,
Under whose conduct half his army went,
The nearest way conducted by the spies;
And he himself, and Edmond Earl of Kent,
 Upon the hill in sight of Burton lay,
 Watching to take advantage of the day.

30.

Stay, Surrey, stay, thou mayst too soon be gone,
Pause till this heat be somewhat overpast,
Full little know'st thou whither thou dost run,
Richmond and Pembroke never make such haste,
Ye do but strive to bring more horror on ;
Never seek sorrow, for it comes too fast.
    Why strive ye thus to pass this fatal flood,
    To fetch but wounds and shed your nearest blood?

31.

Great Lancaster, yet sheathe thy angry sword,
On Edward's arms whose edge thou shouldst not set,
Thy natural kinsman, and thy sovereign lord,
Both from the loins of our Plantagenet ;
Call yet to mind thy once engagéd word :
Canst thou thy oath to Longshanks thus forget ?
    Men should perform before all other things,
    The serious vows they make to God and Kings.

32.

The winds were hushed (no little breath doth blow)
Which seems sate still, as though they listening stood ;
With trampling crowds the very earth doth bow,
And through the smoke the sun appeared like blood ;
What with the shout, and with the dreadful show,
The herds of beasts ran bellowing to the wood,
    When drums and trumpets to the charge did sound,
    As they would shake the gross clouds to the ground.

33.

The Earls then charging with their power of horse,
Taking a signal when they should begin,
Being in view of the imperial force
Which at that time essayed the bridge to win ;
Which made the Barons change their former course,
To avoid the present danger they were in,
　Which on the sudden had they not forecast,
　Of their last day that hour had been the last.

34.

When from the hill the King's main powers come down,
Which had Aquarius to their valiant guide,
Brave Lancaster and Hertford from the town
Do issue forth upon the other side ;
Peer against Peer, the Crown against the Crown,
The King assails, the Barons munified,
　England's red cross upon both sides doth fly,
　"Saint George" the King, "Saint George" the Barons cry.

35.

Like as an exhalation hot and dry,
Amongst the air-bred moisty vapours thrown,
Spitteth his lightning forth outrageously,
Rending the thick clouds with the thunder-stone
Whose fiery splinters through the thin air fly
That with the horror heaven and earth doth groan :
　With the like clamour and confuséd O,
　To the dread shock the desp'rate armies go.

36.

There might men see the famous English bows,
Wherewith our foes we wonted to subdue,
Shoot their sharp arrows in the face of those
Which oft before victoriously them drew;
Yet shun their aim and, troubled in the loose,
Those well-winged weapons, mourning as they flew,
    Slipped from the bowstring impotent and slack,
    As to the archers they would fain turn back.

37.

Behold the remnant of Troy's ancient stock,
Laying on blows as smiths on anvils strike,
Grappling together in the fearful shock
Where still the strong encountereth with the like,
And each as ruthless as the hardened rock,
Were't with the spear, or brown-bill, or the pike,
    Still as the wings or battles came together,
    Ere fortune gave advantage yet to either.

38.

From battered helms with every envious blow
The scattered plumes fly loosely here and there,
To the beholder like to flakes of snow
That ev'ry light breath on its wings doth bear,
As they had sense and feeling of our woe:
And thus affrighted with the sudden fear,
    Now back, now forward, such strange windings make
    As though uncertain which way they should take.

39.

Slaughter alike invadeth either host,
Whilst still the battle strongly doth abide,
Which everywhere runs raking through the coast,
As't pleased outrageous fury it to guide,
Yet not sufficed where tyrannizing most;
So that their wounds, like mouths, by gaping wide,
  Made as they meant to call for present death;
  Had they but tongues, their deepness gives them breath.

40.

Here lies a heap, half slain and partly drowned,
Gasping for breath amongst the slimy segges,
And there a sort laid in a deadly swound,
Trod with the press into the mud and dregs;
Others lie bleeding on the firmer ground,
Hurt in the bodies, maimed of arms and legs:
  One sticks his foe, his scalp another cuts,
  One's feet entangled in another's guts.

41.

One his assailing enemy beguiles,
As from the bridge he fearfully doth fall,
Crushed with his weight upon the stakes and piles;
Some in their gore upon the pavement sprawl;
Our native blood our native earth defiles,
And dire destruction overwhelmeth all;
  Such hideous shrieks the bedlam soldiers breathe,
  As the damned spirits had howled from beneath.

42.

The faction still defying Edward's might,
Edmond of Woodstock, with the men of Kent
Charging afresh, renews the doubtful fight
Upon the Barons, languishing and spent,
Bringing new matter for a tragic sight;
Forth against whom their skilful warriors went,
   Bravely to end what bravely did begin,
   Their noblest spirits will quickly lose or win.

43.

As before Troy bright Thetis' godlike son
Talbot himself in this fierce conflict bare;
Mowbray in fight him matchless honour won;
Clifford for life seemed little but to care;
Audley and Elmsbridge peril scorn to shun;
Gifford seemed danger to her teeth to dare;
   Nor Badlesmer gave back to Edward's power,
   As though they strove whom death should first devour.

44.

I'll not commend thee, Mountfort, nor thee, Teis,
Else your high valour much might justly merit;
Nor, Denvil, dare I whisper of thy praise,
Nor, Willington, will I applaud thy spirit,
Your facts forbid that I your fame should raise;
Nor, Damory, thy due mayst thou inherit:
   Your bays must be your well-deservéd blame,
   For your ill actions quench my sacred flame.

45.

O, had you fashioned your great deeds by them
Who summoned Acon with an English drum ;
Or theirs before, that to Jerusalem
Went with the general power of Christendom:
Then had ye wrought Fame's richest diadem,
As they who fought to free the Saviour's tomb,
  And like them had immortalized your names,
  Where now my song can be but of your shames.

46.

O age inglorious, arms untimely borne,
When that apprové d and victorious shield
Must in this civil massacre be torn,
Bruised with the blows of many a foreign field ;
And more, in this sad overthrow be worn
By those in flight enforced it up to yield !
  For which, since then, the stones for very dread
  Against rough storms cold drops for tears do shed.

47.

When soon King Edward's faint and wavering
    friends,
Which had this while stood doubtfully to pause,
When they perceive that destiny intends
That his success shall justify his cause,
Each in himself fresh courage apprehends,
(For victory both fear and friendship draws)
  And smile on him on whom they late did frown,
  All lend their hands to hew the conquered down.

48.

That scarce a man, which Edward late did lack,
Whilst the proud Barons bare an upright face,
But, when they saw that they had turned their back,
Joins with the King to prosecute their chase,
The Baronage so headlong goes to wrack :
In the just trial of so near a case,
    Enforced to prove the fortune of the coast,
    The day at Burton that had clearly lost.

49.

And to the aid of the victorious King
(Which more and more gave vigour to his hope,
With good success him still encouraging,
And to his actions lent an ampler scope),
Sir Andrew Herckley happily doth bring
On their light horse a valiant Northern troop,
    Armed but too aptly, and with too much speed,
    Most to do harm, when least thereof was need.

50.

When still the Barons, making forth their way,
Through places best for their advantage known,
Retain their army, bodied as they may,
By their defeat far weaker that was grown ;
In their best skill devising day by day,
To offend the assailant, and defend their own,
    Of their mishaps the utmost to endure,
    If nothing else their safety might assure.

51.

In their sad flight, with fury followed thus,
Tracing the North through many a tiresome strait,
And forced through many a passage perilous,
To Burrowbridge, led by their luckless fate ;
Bridges should seem to Barons ominous,
For there they lastly were precipitate ;
   Which place the mark of their mischance doth bear,
   For since that time grass never prospered there.

52.

Where, for new bloodshed they new battles ranged,
And take new breath, to make destruction new ;
Changed is their ground, but yet their fate unchanged,
Which too directly still doth them pursue,
Nor are they and their miseries estranged,
To their estates though they mere strangers grew ;
   The only hope whereon they do depend,
   With courage is to consummate their end.

53.

Like as a herd of overheated deer,
By hot-spurred hunters laboured to be caught,
With hues and hounds recovered everywhere,
Whenas they find their speed avails them naught,
Upon the toils run headlong without fear,
With noise of hounds and holloas as distraught :
   Even so the Barons, in this desperate case,
   Turn upon those which lately did them chase.

54.

Ensign beards ensign, sword 'gainst sword doth
shake,
Drum brawls with drum, as rank doth rank oppose,
There's not a man that care of life doth take,
But Death in earnest to his business goes,
A general havoc as of all to make,
And with destruction doth them all enclose ;
   Dealing itself impartially to all,
   Friend by his friend, as foe by foe, doth fall.

55.

Yet the brave Barons, whilst they do respire,
(In spite of fortune, as they stood prepared)
With courage charge, with comeliness retire,
Make good their ground, and then relieve their guard,
Withstand the enterer, then pursue the flyer,
New form their battle, shifting every ward.
   As your high skill were but your quarrel good,
   O noble spirits, how dear had been your blood !

56.

That well-armed band ambitious Herckley led,
Of which the Barons never dreamt before,
Then greatly stood King Edward's power in stead,
And in the fight assailed the enemy sore :
O day most fatal, and most full of dread !
Never can time thy ruinous waste restore :
   Which with his strength though he attempt to do,
   Well may he strive for, and yet fail of too.

57.

Pale Death beyond his wonted bounds doth swell,
Carving proud flesh in cantles out at large ;
As leaves in autumn, so the bodies fell
Under sharp steel at every boist'rous charge :
O, what sad pen can their destruction tell,
Where scalps lay beaten like the battered targe ?
   And every one he claimeth as his right,
   Whose luck it was not to escape by flight.

58.

Those warlike ensigns waving in the field,
Which lately seemed to brave the embattled foe,
Longer not able their own weight to wield,
Their lofty tops to the base dust do bow :
Here sits a helmet, and there lies a shield,
O, ill did Fate those ancient arms bestow,
   Which as a quarry on the soiled earth lay,
   Seized on by conquest, as a glorious prey.

59.

Where noble Bohun, that most princely peer,
Hertford much honoured, and of high desert,
And to this nation none as he so dear,
Passing the bridge with a resolvéd heart,
To stop his soldiers, which retiring were,
Was 'twixt two planks slain through his lower part :
   But Lancaster, not destined there to die,
   Taken, reserved to further misery.

60.

Whose tragic scene some Muse vouchsafe to sing:
His, of five earldoms who then lived possest,
A brother, son, and uncle to a king,
With favour, friends, and with abundance blest:
What could man think, or could devise the thing,
That but seemed wanting to his worldly rest?
    But on this earth what's free from Fortune's power?
    What an age got, is lost in half an hour.

61.

Some few themselves in sanctuaries hide,
Which, though they have the mercy of the place,
Yet are their bodies so unsanctified,
As that their souls can hardly hope for grace;
Where they in fear and penury abide
A poor dead life, which lengtheneth but a space:
    Hate stands without, whilst horror still within
    Prolongs their shame, yet pardoneth not their sin.

62.

Nor was Death then contented with the dead,
Of full revenge as though it were denied,
And till it might have that accomplishéd,
It held itself in nothing satisfied;
And with delays no longer to be fed,
An unknown torment further doth provide,
    That dead men should in misery remain,
    To make the living die with greater pain.

63.

Ye sovereign cities of this woful isle,
In cypress wreaths and your most sad attire,
Prepare yourselves to build the funeral pile,
Lay your pale hands to this exequious fire,
All mirth and comfort from your streets exile,
Filled with the groans of men when they expire :
　The noblest blood approaching to be shed,
　That ever dropt from any of your dead.

64.

When Thomas Earl of Lancaster, that late
The rebellious Barons traitorously retained,
As the chief agent in this great debate,
Was for the same, ere many days, arraigned,
'Gainst whom at Pomfret they articulate
To whom those treasons chiefly appertained ;
　Whose proofs apparent, so well, nay, ill sped,
　As from his shoulders wrest his reverend head.

65.

Yet Lancaster, it is not thy lost breath
That can assure the safety of the Crown,
Or that can make a covenant with death
To warrant Edward what he thinks his own ;
But he must pay the forfeit of his faith,
When they shall rise which he hath trodden down ;
　All's not a man's that is from others rackt,
　And other agents other ways do act.

66.

Nor was it long, but in that fatal place,
The way to death where Lancaster had led,
But many other in the self-same case,
Him in like manner sadly followéd.
London, would thou hadst had thy former grace,
As thou art first, most blood that thou hadst shed,
　By other cities not exceeded far,
　Whose streets devour the remnant of that war.

67.

O parents, ruthful and heartrending sight!
To see that son that your soft bosoms fed,
His mother's joy, his father's sole delight,
That with much cost yet with more care was bred:
O spectacle, even able to affright
A senseless thing, and terrify the dead!
　His dear, dear blood upon the cold earth poured,
　His quartered corse of crows and kites devoured.

68.

But 'tis not you that here complain alone,
Or to yourselves this fearful portion share;
Here's strange and choice variety of moan,
Poor orphans' tears with widows' mixéd are,
With many friends' sigh, many maidens' groan,
So innocent, so simply pure and rare,
　As Nature, which till then had silence kept,
　Near burst with sorrow, bitterly had wept.

69.

O bloody age ! had not these things been done,
I had not now in these more calmer times,
Into the search of those past troubles run ;
Nor had my virgin unpolluted rhymes
Altered the course wherein they first begun,
To sing these horrid and unnatural crimes ;
  My lays had still been of Idea's bower,
  Of my dear Ancor, or her lovéd Stour.

70.

Nor other subject than yourself had chose,
Your birth, your virtues, and your high respects,
Whose bounties oft have nourished my repose ;
You, whom my Muse ingeniously elects,
Denying earth your brave thoughts to enclose,
Maugre the Momists and Satiric sects ;
  That whilst my verse to after-times is sung,
  You may live with me, and be honoured long.

71.

But greater things my subject hath in store
Still to her task my arméd Muse to keep,
And offereth her occasion as before
Whereon she may in mournful verses weep ;
And as a ship being gotten near the shore,
By awkward winds re-driven to the deep,
  So is the Muse, from whence she came of late,
  Into the business of a troubled State.

THE THIRD CANTO.

THE ARGUMENT.

By sleepy potions that the Queen ordains,
Lord Mortimer escapes out of the Tower;
And by false sleights and many subtle trains,
She gets to France, to raise a foreign power:
The French King leaves his sister; need constrains
The Queen to Hainault in a happy hour;
   Edward her son to Philip is affied,
   They for invasion instantly provide.

1.

SCARCE had these passéd miseries an end,
But other troubles instantly began;
As mischief doth new matter apprehend,
By things that still irregularly ran:
For further yet their fury doth extend,
All was not yielded that King Edward won:
   And some there were in corners that did lie,
   Which o'er his actions had a watchful eye.

2.

Whenas the King, whilst things thus fairly went,
Who by this happy victory grew strong,
Summoned at York a solemn Parliament
To uphold his right, and help the Spensers' wrong
(In all affairs to establish his intent),
Whence more and more his minions' greatness sprung,
   Whose counsels still in ev'ry business crost
   The enragéd Queen, in all misfortunes tost.

3.

Whenas the eld'st, a man extremely hated,
(Whom till that time the King could not prefer
Until he had the Barons' pride abated)
That Parliament made Earl of Winchester,
As Herckey Earl of Carlisle he created:
And likewise Baldock he made Chancellor;
 One whom the King had for his purpose wrought,
 A man, as subtle, so corrupt and nought.

4.

Whenas mishaps, that seldom come alone,
Thick in the necks of one another fell,
The Scot began a new invasion,
And France did thence the English powers expel;
The Irish set the English pale upon,
At home the commons every day rebel:
 Mischief on mischief, curse doth follow curse,
 One ill scarce past, but after comes a worse.

5.

For Mortimer that wind most fitly blew,
Troubling their eyes which otherwise might see,
Whilst the wise Queen, who all advantage knew,
Was closely casting how to set him free;
And did the plot so seriously pursue
Till she had found the means how it should be,
 Against opinion and imperious might,
 To work her own ends through the jaws of spite.

6.

And to that purpose she a potion made,
In operation of that poisoning power,
That it the spirits could presently invade,
And quite dissense the senses in an hour
With such cold numbness, as it might persuade
That very death the patient did devour
 For certain hours, and sealéd up the eyes,
 'Gainst all that art could possibly devise..

7.

In which, she plantain and cold lettuce had,
The water-lily from the marish ground,
With the wan poppy, and the nightshade sad,
And the short moss that on the trees is found,
The pois'ning henbane, and the mandrake drad,
With cypress flowers that with the rest were pound;
 The brain of cranes amongst the rest she takes,
 Mixed with the blood of dormice and of snakes.

8.

Thus, like Medea, sate she in her cell,
Which she had circled with her potent charms,
From thence all hindrance clearly to expel;
Then her with magic instruments she arms,
And to her business instantly she fell:
A vestal fire she lights, wherewith she warms
 The mixéd juices, from those simples wrung,
 To make the med'cine wonderfully strong.

9.

The sundry fears that from her fact might rise,
Men may suppose, her trembling hand might stay,
Had she considered of the enterprise,
To think what peril in the attempt there lay;
Knowing besides, that there were secret spies
Set by her foes to watch her every way:
  But when that sex leave virtue to esteem,
  Those greatly err, which think them what they seem.

10.

Their plighted faith they at their pleasure leave,
Their love is cold, but hot as fire their hate,
On whom they smile they surely those deceive,
In their desires they be insatiate:
Them of their will there's nothing can bereave,
Their anger hath no bound, revenge no date:
  They lay by fear when they at ruin aim,
  They shun not sin, as little weigh they shame.

11.

The elder of the Mortimers this while,
That their sure friends so many sundry ways,
By fight, by execution, by exile,
Had seen cut off, then finishéd his days:
Which, though with grief, doth somewhat reconcile
The younger's thoughts, and lends his cares some ease:
  Which oft his heart, oft troubled had his head,
  For the dear safety of his uncle dead.

12.

But there was more did on his death depend
Than Heaven was pleased the foolish world should
    know;
And why the Fates thus hasted on his end,
Thereby intending stranger plagues to show.
Brave lord, in vain thy breath thou didst not spend;
From thy corruption greater conflicts grow,
    Which began soon and fruitfully to spring,
    New kinds of vengeance on that age to bring.

13.

As heart could wish, when everything was fit,
The Queen attends her potion's power to prove;
Their steadfast friends their best assisting it,
Their trusty servants seal up all in love:
And Mortimer, his valour and his wit
Then must express, whom most it doth behove:
    Each place made sure, where guides and horses lay,
    And where the ship that was for his convey.

14.

Whenas his birthday he had yearly kept,
And used that day those of the Tower to feed;
And on the warders other bounties heapt,
For his advantage he that day decreed,
Which did suspicion clearly intercept,
And much availed him at that time of need
    When after cates, their thirst at last to quench,
    He mixed their liquor with that sleepy drench.

15.

Which soon each sense doth with dead coldness
  seize,
When he, which knew the keepers of each ward,
Out of their pockets quickly took the keys,
His corded ladders readily prepared ;
And stealing forth through dark and secret ways
(Not then to learn his compass by the card)
  To win the walls courageously doth go,
  Which looked as scorning to be mastered so.

16.

They soundly sleep, whilst his quick spirits awake,
Exposed to peril in the highest extremes,
Alcides labours as to undertake,
O'er walls, o'er gates, through watches, and through
  streams,
By which his own way he himself must make :
And let them tell King Edward of their dreams.
  For ere they came out of their brain-sick trance
  He made no doubt to be arrived in France.

17.

The sullen night had her black curtain spread,
Lowering that day had tarried up so long,
And that the morrow might lie long a-bed,
She all the heaven with dusky clouds had hung :
Cynthia plucked in her newly hornéd head,
Away to west, and under earth she flung,
  As she had longed to certify the sun,
  What in his absence in our world was done.

18.

The lesser lights, like sentinels in war,
Behind the clouds stood privily to pry,
As though unseen they subtly strove from far
Of his escape the manner to descry;
Hid was each wand'ring as each fixed star,
As they had held a council in the sky
    And had concluded with that present night,
    That not a star should once give any light.

19.

In a slow silence all the shores are hushed,
Only the screech-owl sounded to the assault,
And Isis with a troubled murmur rushed,
As if consenting, and would hide the fault;
And as his foot the sand or gravel crushed,
There was a little whispering in the vault,
    Moved by his treading, softly as he went,
    Which seemed to say it furthered his intent.

20.

Whilst that wise Queen, whom care yet restless kept,
For happy speed to Heaven held up her hands,
With worlds of hopes and fears together heapt
In her full bosom, listening as she stands;
She sighed and prayed, and sighed again and wept,
She sees him how he climbs, how swims, how lands:
    Though absent, present in desires they be,
    Our soul much farther than our eyes can see.

21

The small clouds issuing from his lips, she saith,
Labouring so fast as he the ladder clame,
Should purge the air of pestilence and death ;
And as from Heaven that filched Promethean flame,
The sweetness so, and virtue of his breath
New creatures in the element should frame,
   And to what part it had the hap to stray,
   There should it make another Milky Way.

22.

Attained the top, whilst spent, he paused to blow,
She saw how round he cast his longing eyes,
The earth to greet him gently from below,
How greatly he was favoured of the skies :
She saw him mark the way he was to go,
And towards her palace how he turned his eyes;
   From the walls' height, as when he down did slide,
   She heard him cry, " Now Fortune be my guide."

23.

As he descended, so did she descend,
As she would hold him that he should not fall,
On whom alone her safety did depend ;
But when some doubt did her deep thoughts appal,
Distractedly she did her hands extend
For speedy help, and earnestly did call
   Softly again, if death to him should hap,
   She begged of Heaven his grave might be her lap.

24.

To show him favour, she entreats the air,
For him she begged the mercy of the wind,
For him she kneeled before the night with prayer,
For him herself she to the earth inclined,
For him, his tides beseeching Thames to spare,
And to command his billows to be kind,
    And tells the flood, if he her love would quit,
    No flood of her should honoured be but it.

25.

But when she thought she saw him swim along,
Doubting the stream was taken with his love,
She feared the drops that on his tresses hung,
And that each wave which most should woo him strove
To his clear body that so closely clung,
Which when before him with his breast he drove,
    Pallid with grief, she turned away her face,
    Jealous that he the waters should embrace.

26.

That angry lion having slipped his chain,
As in a fever made King Edward quake;
Who knew, before he could be caught again,
Dear was the blood that his strong thirst must slake:
He found much labour had been spent in vain,
And must be forced a further course to take,
    Perceiving tempests rising in the wind,
    Of which too late too truly he divined.

27.

By his escape that adverse part grown proud,
On each hand working for a second war,
And in their councils nothing was allowed
But what might be a motive to some jar ;
And though their plots were carried in a cloud
From the discerning of the popular,
    The wiser yet, whose judgments farther wrought,
    Easily perceive how things about were brought.

28.

Those secret fires, by envious faction blown,
Brake out in France, which covered long had lain ;
King Charles from Edward challenging his own,
First Guyne, next Pontieu, and then Aquitain,
To each of which he made his title known,
Nor from their seizure longer would abstain :
    The cause thereof lay out of most men's view,
    Which though fools found not, wise men quickly
        knew.

29.

Their projects hitting many a day in hand,
That to their purpose prosp'rously had thrived,
The base whereon a mighty frame must stand,
By all their cunnings that had been contrived ;
Finding their actions were so throughly manned,
Their fainting hopes were wondrously revived ;
    They made no doubt, to see in little time
    The full of that which then was in the prime.
                                                            c

30.

The King, much troubled with the French affair,
Which, as a shapeless and unwieldy mass,
Wholly employed the utmost of his care
To Charles of France his embassy to pass,
For which it much behoved him to prepare
Before the war too deeply settled was:
    Which, when they found, they likewise cast about,
    As they would go, to make him send them out.

31.

Which, when they came in council to debate,
And to the depth had seriously discussed,
Finding how nearly it concerned the State
To stay a war both dangerous and unjust,
That weighty business to negotiate
They must find one of special worth and trust:
    Where every lord his censure freely past
    Of whom he liked, the Bishop was the last.

32.

Torlton,—whose tongue men's ears in chains could tie
And like Jove's fearful thunderbolt could pierce,
In which there more authority did lie
Than in those words the Sibyls did rehearse
Whose sentence was so absolute and high,
As had the power a judgment to reverse,—
    For the wise Queen, with all his might did stand,
    To lay that charge on her well-guiding hand.

33.

Urging what credit she the cause might bring,
Impartial 'twixt a husband and a brother,
A Queen in person betwixt King and King;
And more than that, to show herself a mother
There for her son, his right establishing,
Which did as much concern them as the other:
  Which colour served to work, in this extreme,
  That of which then the King did never dream.

34.

Torlton, was this thy spiritual pretence?
Would God thy thoughts had been spiritual,
Or less persuasive thy great eloquence:
But O! thy actions were too temporal,
Thy knowledge had too much pre-eminence,
Thy reason subtle and sophistical.
  But all's not true that supposition saith,
  Nor have the mightiest arguments most faith.

35.

Nor did the Bishop those his learnèd lack,
As well of power as policy and wit,
That were prepared his great design to back,
And could amend where aught he did omit:
For with such cunning they had made their pack,
That it went hard if that they should not hit
  That the fair Queen to France with speed must go,
  Hard had he plied, that had persuaded so.

C 2

36.

When she was fitted both of wind and tide,
And saw the coast was every way so clear,
As a wise woman she her business plied,
Whilst things went current, and well carried were,
Herself and hers to get abroad she hied
As one whose fortune made her still to fear:
  Knowing those times so variously inclined,
  And every toy soon altering Edward's mind.

37.

Her followers such as merely friendless stood,
Sunk and dejected by the Spensers' pride,
Who bore the taints of treason in their blood
And for revenge would leave no ways untried,
Whose means were bad, but yet their minds were good
When now at hand they had their help descried;
  Nor were they wanting mischief to invent,
  To work their wills and further her intent.

38.

Whilst Mortimer (that all this while hath lain
From our fair course) by fortune strangely crost,
In France was struggling how he might regain
That which before in England he had lost,
And all good means doth gladly entertain,
No jot dismayed in all those tempests tost;
  Nor his great mind could so be overthrown,
  All men his friends, all countries were his own.

39.

Then Muse, transported by thy former zeal,
Led in thy progress, where his fortune lies,
To thy sure aid I seriously appeal ;
To show him fully, without feigned disguise,
The ancient Heroes then I shall reveal,
And in their patterns I shall be precise,
   When in my verse, transparent, neat and clear,
   They shall in his pure character appear.

40.

He was a man, then boldly dare to say,
In whose rich soul the virtues well did suit,
In whom so mixed the elements all lay,
That none to one could sov'reignty impute,
As all did govern yet all did obey :
He of a temper was so absolute,
   As that it seemed, when Nature him began,
   She meant to show all that might be in man.

41.

So throughly seasoned, and so rightly set,
That in the level of the clearest eye
Time never touched him with deforming fret,
Nor had the power to warp him but awry ;
Whom in his course no cross could ever let,
His elevation fixéd was so high
   That those rough storms, whose rage the world
      doth prove,
   Never wrought him, who sate them far above.

42.

Which the Queen saw, who had a seeing spirit,
For she had marked the largeness of his mind
And with much judgment looked into his merit,
Above the usual compass of her kind,
His grandsires' greatness rightly to inherit
Whenas the ages in their course inclined,
   And the world, weak with time, began to bow
   To that poor baseness that it rests at now.

43.

He weighs not wealth, nor yet his Wigmore left,
Let needless heaps, as things of nothing stand,
That was not his that man could take by theft,
He was a lord if he had sea or land,
And thought him rich of those who was not reft;
Man of all creatures hath an upright hand,
   And by the stars is only taught to know,
   That as they progress heaven, he earth should do.

44.

Wherefore wise Nature from this face of ground
Into the deep taught man to find the way,
That in the floods her treasure might be found,
To make him search for what she there did lay;
And that her secrets he might throughly sound,
She gave him courage, as her only key,
   That of all creatures as the worthiest he
   Her glory there and wondrous works should see.

45.

Let wretched worldlings sweat for mud and earth,
Whose grovelling bosoms lick the recreant stones,
Such peasants cark for plenty and for dearth,
Fame never looks upon those prostrate drones;
The brave mind is allotted in the birth
To manage empires from the state of thrones,
    Frighting coy fortune, when she stern'st appears,
    Which scorneth sighs and jeereth at our tears.

46.

But when report, as with a trembling wing,
Tickled the entrance of his listening ear,
With news of ships sent out the Queen to bring,
For her at Sandwich which then waiting were,
He surely thought he heard the angels sing
And the whole frame of Heaven make up the choir,
    That his full soul was smothered with excess,
    Her ample joys unable to express.

47.

Quoth he, " Slide billows smoothly for her sake,
Whose sight can make your aged Nereus young,
For her fair passage even alleys make,
And as the soft winds waft her sails along,
Sleek every little dimple of the lake,
Sweet Syrens, and be ready with your song;
    Though 'tis not Venus that doth pass that way,
    Yet is as fair as she borne on the sea.

48.

"Ye scaly creatures, gaze upon her eye,
And never after with your kind make war;
O steal the accents from her lips that fly,
Which like the tunes of the Celestials are,
And them to your sick amorous thoughts apply,
Compared with which, Arion's did but jar:
    Wrap them in air, and when black tempests rage,
    Use them as charms the rough seas to assuage.

49.

"France, send to attend her with full shoals of oars,
With which her fleet may every way be plied;
And when she landeth on thy blessèd shores,
And the vast navy doth at anchor ride
For her departure, when the wild sea roars,
Ship mount to heaven, and there be stellified:
    Next Jason's Argo, on the burnished throne,
    Assume thyself a constellation."

50.

Queen Isabel then landing with delight,
Had what rich France could lend her for her ease;
And as she passed, no town but did invite
Her with some show, her appetite to please:
But Mortimer once coming in her sight,
His shape and features did her fancy seize;
    When she, that knew how her fit time to take,
    Thus she her most loved Mortimer bespake:

51.

"O Mortimer, sweet Mortimer," quoth she,
"What angry power did first the means devise
To separate Queen Isabel and thee,
Whom to despite love yet together ties?
But if thou think'st the fault was made by me,
For a just penance to my longing eyes,
　　Though guiltless they, this be to them assigned,
　　To gaze upon thee till they leave me blind.

52.

"My dear, dear heart, thought I to see thee thus,
When first in Court thou didst my favour wear,
When we have watched, lest any noted us,
Whilst our looks used love's messages to bear,
And we by signs sent many a secret buss,
An exile then, thought I to see thee here?
　　But what couldst thou be then, but now thou art?
　　Though banished England, yet not from my heart.

53.

"That fate which did thy franchisement enforce,
And from the depth of danger set thee free,
Still regular and constant in that course,
Made me this straight and even path to thee;
Of our affections as it took remorse,
Our birth-fixed stars so luckily agree,
　　Whose revolution seriously directs
　　Our like proceedings to the like effects.

54.

"Only wise counsel hath contrived this thing,
For which we wished so many a woful day,
Of which the clear and perfect managing
Is that strong prop, whereon our hopes may stay;
Which in itself the authority doth bring
That weak opinion hath not power to sway,
   Confuting those whose sightless judgments sit
   In the thick rank with ev'ry common wit.

55.

"Then since the essáy our good success affords,
And we her fav'rites lean on Fortune's breast,
That every hour new comfort us procures,
Of these her blessings let us choose the best;
And whilst the day of our good hap endures,
Let's take the bounteous benefits of rest:
   Let's fear no storm before we feel a shower,
   My son a King, two kingdoms help my dower.

56.

"Of wanton Edward when I first was wooed,
Why cam'st thou not into the Court of France?
Before thy King thou in my grace hadst stood;
O Mortimer, how good had been thy chance!
My love attempted in that youthful mood,
I might have been thine own inheritance;
   Where entering now by force thou hold'st by might,
   And art disseisor of another's right.

57.

"Thou idol, Honour, which we fools adore,
How many plagues do rest in thee to grieve us!
Which when we have, we find there is much more
Than that which only is a name can give us;
Of real comforts thou dost leave us poor,
And of those joys thou often dost deprive us,
    That with ourselves doth set us at debate,
    And makes us beggars in our greatest state."

58.

With such brave raptures from her words that rise,
She made a breach in his impressive breast,
And all his powers so fully did surprise
As seemed to rock his senses to their rest,
So that his wit could not that thing devise
Of which he thought his soul was not possest:
    Whose great abundance, like a swelling flood
    After a shower, ran through his ravished blood.

59.

Like as a lute, that's touched with curious skill,
Each string stretched up, his right tone to retain,
Music's true language that doth speak at will,
The bass and treble married by the mean,
Whose sounds each note with harmony do fill
Whether it be in descant or on plain,
    So their affections, set in keys alike,
    In true consent meet, as their humours strike.

60.

As the plain path to their design appears,
Of whose wished sight they had been long debarred;
By the dissolving of those threatening fears
That many a purpose, many a plot had marred,
Their hope at full, so heartily them cheers,
And their protection by a stronger guard
    Lends them that leisure, the events to cast
Of things to come by those already past.

61.

For this great business easily setting out,
By due proportion measuring every pace,
To avoid the cumbrance of each hindering doubt
And not to fail of comeliness and grace,
They came with every circumstance about,
Observe the person, as the time and place,
    Nor leave they aught, that in discretion's laws,
They could but think might beautify the cause.

62.

Their embassy delivering in that height
As of the same the dignity might fit,
Apparelling a matter of that weight
In ceremony well beseeming it;
And that it should go steadily and right
They at their audience no one point omit,
    As to the full each tittle to effect,
That in such cases wisdom should respect.

63.

Nor to negotiate never do they cease
Till they again that ancient league combine ;
Yet so, that Edward should his right release,
And to his son the Provinces resign,
With whom King Charles concludes the happy peace,
Having the homage due to him for Guine ;
    And that both realms should ratify their deed,
    They for both Kings an interview decreed.

64.

Yet in this thing, which all men thought so plain,
And to have been accomplished with such care,
Their inward falsehood hidden did remain,
Quite from the colour that the outside bare :
For only they this interview did gain,
To entrap the King, so trainéd to their snare :
    For which they knew that he must pass the seas,
    Or else the Prince, which better would them please.

65.

Which by the Spensers was approvéd, who
(As in his councils they did chiefly guide)
With him their sovereign, nor to France durst go,
Nor in his absence durst at home abide ;
Whilst the weak King stood doubtful what to do,
His listening ears they with persuasions plied,
    That he to stay was absolutely won,
    And for that business to despatch his son.

66.

Thus is the King encompassed by their skill,
And made to act what Torlton did devise,
Who thrust him on, to draw them up the hill,
That by his strength they might get power to rise,
For they in all things were before him still :
That perfect steersman in all policies
    Had cast to walk where Edward bare the light,
    And by his aim he levelléd their sight.

67.

Thus having made what Edward most did will
For his advantage further their intent,
With seeming good so varnishing their ill
That it went current by the fair event,
And of their hopes the utmost to fulfil,
Things in their course came in so true consent,
    To bring their business to that happy end,
    That they the same might publicly defend.

68.

The precious time no longer they protract,
Nor in suspense their friends at home do hold,
Being abroad so absolutely backed,
They quickly waxéd confident and bold,
In their proceeding publishing their act ;
Nor did they fear to whom report it told,
    But with an arméd and erected hand
    To abet their own did absolutely stand.

69.

And that base Bishop then of Exeter,
A man experienced in their councils long,
Thinking perhaps his falsehood might prefer
Him, or else movéd with King Edward's wrong,
Or whether that his frailty made him err,
Or other fatal accident among:
  But he from France and them to England flew,
  And knowing all, discovered all he knew.

70.

Their treasons long in hatching thus disclosed,
And Torlton's drift by circumstances found,
With what conveyance things had been disposed,
The cunning used in casting of their ground,
The frame as fit in every point composed,
When better counsel coldly came to sound,
  Awaked the King to see his weak estate,
  When the prevention came a day too late.

71.

Yet her departing whilst she doth adjourn,
Charles, as a brother, by persuasion deals,
Edward with threats would force her to return;
Pope John her with his dreadful curse assails:
But all in vain against her will they spurn,
Persuasion, threat, nor curse with her prevails:
  Charles, Edward, John, strive all to do your worst,
  The Queen fares best when she the most is curst.

72.

Which to the Spensers speedily made seen,
With what clean sleight things had been brought about,
And that those here, which well might ruled have been,
Quickly had found that they were gotten out,
And knowing well their wit, their power, and spleen,
Of their own safeties much began to doubt,
   And therefore must some present means invent,
   To avoid a danger, else most imminent.

73.

When they, who had the Frenchmen's humours felt
And knew the bait wherewith they might be caught,
By promise of large pensions with them dealt
If that King Charles might from her aid be wrought:
What mind so hard, that money cannot melt?
Which they to pass in little time had brought;
   That Isabel, too easily over-weighed
   By their great sums, was frustrate of her aid.

74.

Yet could not this amaze that mighty Queen,
Whom sad affliction never had controlled,
Never such courage in that sex was seen,
She was not cast in other women's mould,
Nor could rebate the edge of her high spleen,
Who could endure war, travel, want, and cold,
   Struggling with fortune, ne'er by her opprest,
   Most cheerful still when she was most distrest.

75.

But then resolved to leave ungrateful France
And in the world her better fate to try,
Changing the air, hopes time may alter chance,
Under her burthen scorning so to lie,
Her weakened state still striving to advance,
Her mighty mind flew in a pitch so high :
   Yet ere she went, her vexed heart that did ache,
   Somewhat to ease, thus to the King she spake :

76.

" Is this a King's, a brother's part ? " quoth she,
" And to this end did I my grief unfold ?
Came I, to heal my wounded heart, to thee
Where slain outright I now the same behold ?
Be these thy vows, thy promises to me ?
In all this heat art thou become so cold
   To leave me thus forsaken at the worst,
   My state at last more wretched than at first ?

77.

" Thy wisdom, weighing what my wants require,
To thy dear mercy might my tears have tied,
Our bloods receiving heat both from one fire ;
And we by fortune, as by birth allied,
My suit supported by my just desire,
Were arguments not to have been denied :
   The grievous wrongs that in my bosom be,
   Should be as near thy care as I to thee.

78.

"Nature, too easily working on my sex,
Thus at thy pleasure my poor fortune leaves,
Which being enticed with hopes of due respects
From thee, my trust dishonestly deceives,
Who me and mine unnaturally neglects,
And of all comfort lastly us bereaves,
    What 'twixt thy baseness and thy beastly will,
    To expose thy sister to the worst of ill.

79.

"But for my farewell thus I prophesy,
That from my womb he's sprung, or he shall spring,
Who shall subdue thy next posterity,
And lead a captive thy succeeding King,
The just revenge of thy vile injury:
To fatal France, I as a Sibyl sing
    Her cities' sack, the slaughter of her men,
    Of whom one Englishman shall conquer ten."

80.

The Earl of Hainault, in that season great,
The wealthy lord of many a warlike tower,
Whom for his friendship princes did entreat,
As fearing both his policy and power,
Having a brother wondrously complete,
Called John of Beaumont (in a happy hour,
    As it for the distressèd Queen did chance)
    That time abiding in the Court of France.

81.

He, there the while, this shuffling that had seen,
Whom to her party Isabel had won,
To pass for Hainault humbly prays the Queen,
Prompting her still what good might there be done,
To ease the anguish of her tumorous spleen,
Offering his fair niece to the Prince her son,
   The only way to win his brother's might
   Against the King, to back her in her right.

82.

Who had an ear not filled with his report
To whom the soldiers of that time did throng?
The pattern to all other of his sort,
Well learned in what to honour did belong,
With that brave Queen long trainéd up in Court,
And constantly confirméd in her wrong:
   Besides all this, crossed by the adverse part
   In things that sate too near to his great heart.

83.

Sufficient motives to invite distress
To apprehend so excellent a mean
Against those ills that did so strongly press,
Whereon the Queen her weak estate might lean,
And at that season, though it were the less,
Yet for a while it might her want sustain
   Until the approaching of more prosperous days
   Her drooping hopes to their first height might raise.

84.

When they at large had leisure to debate,
Where welcome looked with a well-pleaséd face
From those dishonours she receivéd late,
For there she wanted no obsequious grace,
Under the guidance of a gentler fate,
All bounteous offers freely they embrace,
   And to conclude, all ceremonies past,
   The Prince affies fair Philip at the last.

85.

All covenants betwixt them surely sealed
Each to the other lastingly to bind,
Nothing but done with equity and zeal,
And suiting well with Hainault's mighty mind
Which to them all did much content reveal ;
The ease the Queen was like thereby to find,
   The comfort coming to the lovely bride,
   Prince Edward pleased, and joy on every side.

THE FOURTH CANTO.

THE ARGUMENT.

The Queen in Hainault mighty friends doth win,
In Harwich Haven safely is arrived,
Garboils in England more and more begin ;
King Edward of his safety is deprived,
Flieth to Wales, at Neath receivéd in,
Whilst many plots against him are contrived :
    Lastly betrayed, the Spensers and his friends
    Are put to death, with which this Canto ends.

1.

Now seven times Phœbus had his welkéd wain
Upon the top of Cancer's tropic set,
And seven times in his descent again,
His fiery wheels had with the Fishes wet,
In the occurrents of King Edward's reign,
Since mischief did these miseries beget ;
    Which through more strange varieties had run
    Than he that while celestial signs had done.

2.

Whilst our ill-thriving in those Scottish broils
Their strength and courage greatly did advance,
In a small time made wealthy by our spoils ;
And we much weakened by our wars in France
Were well near quite disheartened by our foils :
But at these things the Muse must only glance,
    And Herckley's treasons haste to bring to view,
    Her serious subject sooner to pursue.

3.

When Robert Bruce with his brave Scottish band
By other inroads on the Borders made,
Had well near wasted all Northumberland,
Whose towns he level with the earth had laid ;
And finding none his power there to withstand,
On the north part of spacious Yorkshire preyed,
 Bearing away with pride his pillage got,
 As fate to him did our last fall allot.

4.

For which that Herckley by his sovereign sent,
To entreat a needful though dishonoured peace,
Under the colour of a true intent
Kindled the war, in a fair way to cease,
And with King Robert did a course invent
His homage due to Edward to release :
 Besides, their faith they each to other plight,
 In peace and war to join with all their might.

5.

Yet more, King Robert (things being carried so,
His sister to that treach'rous Earl affied,
Which made too plain and evident a show
Of what before his trust did closely hide :
But the cause found, from whence this league
  should grow,
By such as, near, into their actions pryed),
 Discovered treasons, which not quickly crost,
 Had shed more blood than all the wars had cost.

6.

Whether the King's weak councils causes are
That everything so badly falleth out,
Or that the Earl did of our state despair,
When nothing prospered that was gone about,
And therefore careless how the English fare,
I'll not dispute, but leave it as a doubt,
   Or some vain title his ambition lacked,
   But something hatched this treasonable act.

7.

Which once revealéd to the jealous King,
The apprehension of that traitorous Peer
He left to the Lord Lucie's managing,
(One whose proved faith he had held ever dear)
By whose brave carriage in so hard a thing,
He did well worthy of his trust appear :
   Who in his castle, carelessly defended,
   That crafty Carlel closely apprehended.

8.

For which, ere long, to his just trial led,
In all the robes befitting his degree,
Where Scroope, Chief Justice in that dang'rous stead,
Commission had his lawful judge to be :
And on the proofs of his indictment read,
His treasons all so easily might see :
   Which soon themselves so plainly did express,
   As might assure them of his ill success,

9.

His style and titles to the King restored,
Noted with names of infamy and scorn,
And next, disarméd of his knightly sword,
On which before his fealty was sworn,
Then, by a varlet of his spurs disspurred,
His coat of arms, before him, razed and torn ;
   And to the hurdle lastly he was sent,
   To a trait'rous death, that trait'rously had meant.

10.

Whereon the King a Parliament procured,
To fix some things whose fall he else might fear ;
Whereby he hoped the Queen to have abjured,
His son, and such as their adjutors were :
But those of whom himself he most assured
What they had seemed, the same did not appear,
   When he soon found he had his purpose missed,
   For there were those that durst his power resist.

11.

For Hereford, in Parliament accused
Of sundry treasons, wherein he was caught,
By such his courses strictly as perused,
Whereby subversion of the realm was sought,
His holy habit and his trust abused,
Who, to his answer when he should be brought,
   Was by the clergy (in the King's despite)
   Seized, under colour of the Church's right.

12.

When some, the favourers of this fatal war,
Whom this example did more sharply whet,
Those for the cause that then imprisoned were
Boldly attempt at liberty to set ;
Whose purpose frustrate by their enemies' care,
New garboils doth continually beget,
　　Bidding the King with care to look about,
　　Those secret fires so hourly breaking out.

13.

And the Earl of Kent, who was by Edward placed
As the great General of his force in Guyne,
Was in his absence here at home disgraced,
And frustrated both of supplies and coin
By such lewd persons, to maintain their waste,
As from his treasures ceased not to purloin :
　　Nor could the King be moved, so careless still
　　Both of his own loss and his brother's ill.

14.

Whose discontent too quickly being found,
By such as all advantages did wait,
Who still applied strong corsives to the wound,
And by their tricks and intricate deceit
Hindered those means that haply might redound
That fast arising mischief to defeat,
　　Till Edmund's wrongs were to that ripeness grown,
　　That they had made him absolute their own.

15.

With all his faithful followers in those wars,
Men well experienced and of worthiest parts,
Who for their pay receivéd only scars,
Whilst the inglorious had their due deserts,
And minions' hate of other hope debars,
Which vexed them deeply to the very hearts,
  That to their General for revenge they cry,
  Joining with Beaumont, giving him supply.

16.

These great commanders, and with them combin
The Lord Pocelles, Sares, and Boyseers,
Dambretticourt, the young and valiant Heine,
Estotivyle, Comines, and Villeers,
The valiant knights, Sir Michael de la Lyne,
Sir Robert Baliol, Boswit, and Semeers;
  Men of great skill, whom spoil and glory warms,
  Such as, indeed, were dedicate to arms.

17.

Leading three thousand mustered men in pay,
Of French, Scots, Alman, Switzer and the Dutch;
Of native English fled beyond the sea,
Whose number near amounted to as much,
Which long had looked, nay, waited for that day,
Whom their revenge did but too nearly touch,
  Besides, friends ready to receive them in;
  And new commotions ev'ry day begin.

18.

Whilst the wise Queen, from England day by day
Of all those doings that had certain word,
Whose friends much blamed her over-long delay,
Whenas the time such fitness did afford,
Doth for her passage presently purvey,
Bearing provision every hour aboard,
    Ships of all burthens rigged and mannéd are,
    Fit for invasion, to transport a war.

19.

When she for England fairly setting forth,
Spreading her proud sails on the watery plain,
Steereth her course directly to the North,
With her young Edward, Duke of Aquitaine,
With other three, of special name and worth,
The destined scourges of King Edward's reign,
    Her soldier Beaumont, and the Earl of Kent,
    With Mortimer, that mighty malcontent.

20.

For Harwich Road a fore-wind finely blows,
But blew too fast, to kindle such a fire,
Whilst with full sail and the stiff tide she goes ;
It should have turned and forced her to retire ;
The fleet it drove, was fraughted with our woes,
But seas and winds do Edward's wrack conspire :
    For when just Heaven to chastise us is bent,
    All things convert to our due punishment.

21.

The coasts were kept with a continual ward,
The beacons watched, her coming to descry;
Had but the love of subjects been his guard,
It had been to effect that he did fortify:
But whilst he stood against his foes prepared,
He was betrayed by his home enemy:
    Small help by this he was but like to win,
    Shutting war out, he locked destruction in.

22.

When Henry, brother to that luckless prince,
The first great mover of that civil strife,
Thomas, whom law but lately did convince,
That had at Pomfret left his wretched life;
That Henry, in whose bosom ever since
Revenge lay covered, watching for relief,
    Like fire in some fat mineral of the earth,
    Finding a fit vent, gives her fury birth.

23.

And being Earl Marshal, great upon that coast,
With bells and bonfires welcomes her ashore;
And by his office gathering up a host,
Showed the great spleen that he to Edward bore,
Nor of the same abashed at all to boast;
The clergy's power, in readiness before,
    And on their friends a tax as freely laid,
    To raise munition for their present aid.

24.

And to confusion all their powers expose
On the rent bosom of the land, which long
War, like the sea, on each side did enclose,
A war from our own home dissensions sprung,
In little time which to that greatness rose,
As made us loathed our neighbouring States among ;
   But this invasion, that they hither brought,
   More mischief far than all the former wrought.

25.

Besides, this innovation in the State
Lent their great action such a violent hand,
When it so boldly durst insinuate
On the cold faintness of the enfeebled land,
That being armed with all the power of fate,
Finding a way so openly to stand,
   To their intendment might, if followed well,
   Regain that height from whence they lately fell.

26.

Their strengths together in this meantime met,
All helps and hurts by war's best counsels weighed,
As what might further, what their course might let,
As their reliefs conveniently they laid,
As where they hoped security to get,
Whereon at worst their fortunes might be stayed,
   So fully furnished as themselves desired
   Of what the action needfully required.

27.

When at Saint Edmund's they a while repose,
To rest themselves and their sea-beaten force,
Better to learn the manner of their foes,
To the end not idly to direct their course,
And seeing daily how their army grows,
To take a full view of their foot and horse,
 With much discretion managing the war,
 To let the world know what to do, they dare.

28.

Whenas the King of their proceedings heard,
And of the routs that daily to them run;
But little strength at London then prepared,
Where he had hoped most favour to have won:
He left the City to the watchful guard
Of his approved, most trusted Stapleton,
 To John of Eltham, his deaf son, the Tower,
 And goes himself towards Wales, to raise him power.

29.

Yet whilst his name doth any hope admit,
He made proclaimed, in pain of goods and life,
Or who would have a subject's benefit
Should bend themselves against his son and wife;
And doth all slaughters generally acquit,
Committed on the movers of this strife;
 As who could bring in Mortimer's proud head
 Should freely take the revenues of the dead.

30.

Which was encountered by the Queen's edict,
By publishing the justness of her cause,
That she proceeded in a course so strict
To uphold their ancient liberties and laws :
And that on Edward she did nought inflict
For private hate or popular applause ;
   Only the Spensers to account to bring,
   Whose wicked counsels had abused the King.

31.

Which ballasted the multitude, that stood
As a bark beaten betwixt wind and tide,
By winds exposed, opposéd by the flood,
Nought therein left, to land the same to guide :
Thus floated they in their inconstant mood
Till that the weakness of King Edward's side
   Suffered a seizure of itself at last,
   Which to the Queen a free advantage cast.

32.

Thus Edward left his England to his foes,
Whom danger did to recreant flight debase,
As far from hope as he was near his woes,
Deprived of princely sovereignty and grace,
Yet still grew less the farther that he goes,
His safety soon suspecting every place :
   No help at home, nor succour seen abroad,
   His mind wants rest, his body safe abode.

33.

One scarce to him his sad discourse hath done
Of Hainault's power and what the Queen intends,
But whilst he speaks, another hath begun :
A third then takes it where the second ends,
And tells what rumours through the countries run,
Of those new foes, of those revolted friends:
　Straight came a fourth, in post that thither sped,
　With news of foes come in of friends outfled.

34.

What plagues did Edward for himself prepare ?
Forsaken King, O whither didst thou fly !
Changing the clime, thou couldst not change thy care.
Thou fledst thy foes, but followedst misery :
Those evil lucks in numbers many are
That to thy footsteps do themselves apply ;
　And still, thy conscience corrosived with grief,
　Thou but pursuest thyself, both robbed and thief.

35.

Who seeking succour, offered next at hand,
At last for Wales he takes him to the seas,
And seeing Lundy that so fair did stand,
Thither would steer to give his sorrows ease ;
That little model of his greater land,
As in a dream his fancy seemed to please :
　For fain he would be King yet of an isle,
　Although his empire bounded in a mile.

36.

But when he thought to strike his prosperous sail,
As under lee, past danger of the flood,
A sudden storm of mixéd sleet and hail,
Not suffereth him to rule that piece of wood:
What doth his labour, what his toil avail,
That is by the Celestial Powers withstood?
   And all his hopes him vainly do delude,
   By God and man incessantly pursued.

37.

In that black tempest long turmoiled and tost,
Quite from his course and well he knew not where,
'Mongst rocks and sands in danger to be lost,
Not in more peril than he was in fear;
At length perceiving he was near some coast,
And that the weather somewhat 'gan to clear,
   He found 'twas Wales; and by the mountains tall
   That part thereof which we Glamorgan call.

38.

In Neath, a castle next at hand, and strong,
Where he commandeth entrance with his crew,
The Earl of Gloucester, worker of much wrong,
His Chancellor Baldock, which much evil knew,
Reding his Marshal, other friends among;
Where closely hid, though not from envy's view,
   The Muse a little leaveth them to dwell,
   And of great slaughter shapes herself to tell.

D

39.

Now lighter humour leave me and be gone,
Your passion poor yields matter much too slight :
To write those plagues that then were coming on,
Doth ask a pen of ebon and the night,
If there be ghosts their murder that bemoan,
Let them approach me and in piteous plight
   Howl, and about me with black tapers stand
   To lend a sad light to my sadder hand.

40.

Each line shall lead to some one weeping woe,
And every cadence as a tortured cry,
Till they force tears in such excess to flow,
That they surround the circle of each eye :
Then whilst these sad calamities I show,
All loose affections stand ye idly by,
   Destined again to dip my pen in gore,
   For the saddest tale that time did e'er deplore.

41.

New sorts of plagues were threatened to the earth,
The raging ocean past his bounds did rise,
Strange apparitions and prodigious birth,
Unheard-of sickness and calamities,
More unaccustomed and unlooked-for dearth,
New sorts of meteors gazing from the skies :
   As what before had small or nothing been,
   And only then their plagues did but begin.

42.

And whilst the Queen did in this course proceed,
The land lay open to all offered ill ;
The lawless exile did return with speed,
Not to defend his country, but to kill ;
Then were the prisons dissolutely freed,
Both field and town with wretchedness to fill ;
   London, as thou wast author of such shame,
   Even so wast thou most plaguéd with the same.

43.

Whose giddy commons, merciless and rude,
Let loose to mischief on that dismal day,
Their hands in blood of Edward's friends imbrued ;
Which in their madness having made away,
The implacable, the monstrous multitude,
On his Lieutenant Stapleton did prey,
   Who dragged by them o'er many a loathsome heap,
   Beheaded was before the Cross in Cheap.

44.

Here first she read upon her ruined wall
Her sad destruction, which was but too nigh,
Upon her gates was charactered her fall,
In mangled bodies her anatomy,
Which for her errors did that reckoning call
As might have wrought tears from her ruthless eye ;
   And if the thick air dimmed her hateful sight,
   Her buildings were on fire, to give her light.

45.

Her channels served for ink, her paper stones,
Whereon to write her murder, incest, rape ;
And for her pens, a heap of dead men's bones
To make each letter in some monstrous shape,
And for her accents, sad departing groans ;
And that to time no desperate act should 'scape,
 If she with pride again should be o'ergone,
 To take that book and sadly look thereon.

46.

The tender girl spoiled of her virgin shame,
Yet for that sin no ravisher was shent ;
Black is my ink, more black was her defame,
None to revenge, scarce any to lament ;
Nought could be done to remedy the same,
It was too late those mischiefs to prevent :
 Against those horrors she did idly strive,
 But saw herself to be devoured alive.

47.

She wants redress, and ravishment remorse,
None would be found to whom she could complain,
And crying out against the adulterer's force
Her plaints untimely did return in vain ;
The more she grieved, her misery the worse :
Only to her this help there did remain,
 She spoiled of fame was prodigal of breath,
 And made her life clear by her resolute death.

48.

Then of that world men did the want complain
When they might have been buried when they died,
Young children safely in their cradles lain,
The man new married have enjoyed his bride,
When in some bounds ill could itself contain,
The son kneeled by his father's death-bed side;
    The living wronged, the dead no rite could have,
    The father saw his son to want a grave.

49.

But 'twas too late those courses to recall,
None have external nor internal fear,
Those deadly sounds by their continual fall
Settle confusion in each deafened ear ;
Of our ill times this was the worst of all,
Only of garboils that did love to hear,
    Arms our attire and wounds were all our good,
    Branded the most with rapine and with blood.

50.

Inglorious age, of whom it should be said,
That all these mischiefs should abound in thee,
That all these sins should to thy charge be laid,
From no calumnious nor vile action free !
O let not time us with those ills upbraid,
Lest fear what hath been argue what may be,
    And fashioning so a habit in the mind,
    Make us alone the haters of our kind !

51.

O powerful Heaven, in whose most sov'reign reign
All thy pure bodies move in harmony,
By thee in an inviolable chain
Together linked, so tied in unity
That they therein continually remain,
Swayed in one certain course eternally:
  Why his true motion keepeth every star,
  Yet what they govern so irregular.

52.

But in the course of this unnatural war,
Muse, say from whence this height of mischief grew
That in so short time spread itself so far,
From whence so sundry bloodsheds did ensue,
The cause, I pray thee, faithfully declare:
What? men, religious, was the fault in you,
  Which resty grown, with your much power, withdraw
  Your stiffened necks from yoke of civil awe?

53.

No wonder though the people grew profane
When churchmen's lives gave laymen leave to fall,
And did their former humbleness disdain;
The shirt of hair turned coat of costly pall,
The holy ephod made a cloak for gain,
What done with cunning was canonical,
  And blind promotion shunned that dangerous road
  Which the old prophets diligently trode.

54.

Hence 'twas that God so slightly was adored,
That Rock removed whereon our faith was grounded,
Conscience esteemed but as an idle word,
And being weak, by vain opinions wounded ;
Professors' lives did little fruit afford,
And, in her sects, Religion lay confounded :
    Most sacred things were merchandise become,
    None talked of texts, but prophesying dumb.

55.

The Church then rich, and with such pride possest,
Was like the poison of infectious air,
That having found a way into the breast,
Is not prescribed, nor long time stays it there,
But through the organs seizeth on the rest,
The rank contagion spreading everywhere :
    So, from that evil by the Church begun,
    The Commonwealth was lastly overrun.

56.

When craft crept in to cancel wholesome laws,
Which fastening once on the defective weal,
Where doubts should cease they rose in ev'ry clause,
And made them hurt which first were made to heal ;
One evil still another forward draws ;
For when disorder doth so far prevail,
    That conscience is cast off as out of use,
    Right is the cloak of wrong and all abuse.

57.

Meanwhile, the King, thus keeping in his hold
(In that his poor imprisoned liberty,
Living a death, in hunger, want, and cold,
Almost beyond imagined misery),
By hateful treason secretly was sold,
Through keys delivered to the enemy:
    For when the oppressed is once up to the chin,
    Quite overhead all help to thrust him in.

58.

The dire disaster of that captived King,
So surely seized on by the adverse part
(To his few friends sad matter menacing)
Struck with pale terror every willing heart,
Their expectation clean discouraging,
Him no evasion left, whereby to start,
    And the black cloud, which greatliest did them fear,
    Rose, where their hopes once brightest did appear.

59.

For first, their envy with unusual force,
Fell on the Spensers, from whose only hate
The war first sprung; who found their lawless course
Drew to an end, confinéd by their fate:
Of whom there was not any took remorse,
But as pernicious cankers of the State,
    The father first, to Bristol being led,
    Was drawn to death, then hanged and quarteréd.

60.

Whenas the heir to Winchester, then dead,
The lot ere long to his son Gloster fell ;
Reding the Marshal the like way was led,
And after him the Earl of Arundel,
To pay the forfeit of a reverend head :
Then Muchelden, and with him Daniel,
   These following him in his lascivious ways,
   Then went before him, to his fatal days.

61.

Like some large pillar of a lordly height,
On whose proud top some huge frame doth depend,
By time disabled to uphold the weight,
And that with age his back begins to bend,
Shrinks to his first seat, and in piteous plight,
The lesser props with his sad load doth spend :
   So fared it with King Edward, crushing all
   That had stood near him in his violent fall.

62.

The State whereon these princes proudly lean,
Whose high ascent men trembling still behold,
From whence ofttimes with insolent disdain
The kneeling subject hears himself controlled,
Their earthly weakness truly doth explain,
Promoting whom they please not whom they should,
   Whenas their fall shows how they foully erred,
   Procured by those whom fondly they preferred.

63.

For when that men of merit go ungraced,
And by her fautors ignorance held in,
And parasites in good men's rooms are placed
Only to soothe the highest in their sin,
From those whose skill and knowledge is debased
There many strange enormities begin :
    For great wits forgéd into factious tools,
    Prove great men oft to be the greatest fools.

64.

But why so vainly time do I bestow,
The base abuse of this vile world to chide?
Whose blinded judgment every hour doth show,
What folly weak mortality doth guide.
Wise was that man who laughed at human woe ;
My subject still more sorrow doth provide,
    And these designs more matter still do breed,
    To hasten that which quickly must succeed.

THE FIFTH CANTO.

THE ARGUMENT.

The imprisoned King his sceptre doth forsake,
To quit himself of what he was accused;
His foes him from the Earl of Leicester take,
Who their commission fain would have refused:
His torturers a mockery of him make,
And basely and reproachfully abused,
   By secret ways to Berkeley he is led,
   And there in prison lastly murderéd.

1.

THE wretched King unnaturally betrayed,
By too much trusting to his native land,
From Neath in Wales to Kenilworth conveyed,
By the Earl of Leicester, with a mighty band;
Some few his favourers quickly over-weighed:
When straight there went a Parliament in hand,
   To ratify the general intent,
   For resignation of his government.

2.

Fallen through his frailty and intemperate will,
That with his fortune it so weakly fared,
To undergo that unexpected ill
For his deservéd punishment prepared
Past measure, as those miseries to fill
To him allotted as his just reward:
   All armed with malice, either less or more,
   To strike at him who struck at all before.

3.

It being a thing the Commons still did crave,
The Barons thereto resolutely bent,
Such happy helps on every side to have,
To forward that their forcible intent,
So perfect speed to their great action gave,
Established by the general consent
    On Edward that such miseries did bring,
    As never were inflicted on a King.

4.

Earls, Bishops, Barons, and the Abbots all,
Each in due order, as became their state,
By heralds placéd in the Castle hall;
The burgesses for places corporate,
Whom the great business at that time did call,
For the Cinque Ports the Barons convocate
    With the Shire knights, for the whole body sent,
    Both for the south and for the north of Trent.

5.

When Edward, clothéd mournfully in black,
Was forth before the great assembly brought,
A doleful hearse upon a dead man's back,
Whose heavy looks expressed his heavy thought,
In which there did no part of sorrow lack,
True grief needs not feigned action to be taught:
    His funeral solemnizéd in his cheer,
    His eyes the mourners and his legs the bier.

6.

Torlton, as one select to that intent,
The best experienced in that great affair,
A man grave, subtle, stout, and eloquent,
First with fair speech the assembly doth prepare;
Then with a grace austere and eminent
Doth his abuse effectually declare,
    Winning each sad eye to a reverend fear,
    To due attention drawing every ear.

7.

Urging the exactions raiséd by the King,
With whose full plenty he his minions fed
Him and his subjects still impoverishing;
And the much blood he lavishly had shed,
A desolation on the land to bring:
As under him how ill all business sped,
    The loss in war, sustainéd through his blame,
    A lasting scandal to the English name.

8.

Withal, proceeding with the future good
That they thereby did happily intend,
And with what upright policy it stood,
No other hopes their fortunes to amend;
The resignation to his proper blood,
That might the action lawfully defend;
    The present want that willed it to be so,
    Whose imposition they might not foreslow.

9.

Much more he spake, but fain would I be short,
To this intent a speech delivering :
Nor may I be too curious to report
What toucheth the deposing of a King :
Wherefore I warn thee, Muse, not to exhort
The after-times to this forbidden thing
  By reasons for it by the Bishop laid,
  Or from my feeling what he might have said.

10.

The grave delivery of whose vehement speech,
Graced with a dauntless, uncontracted brow,
The assembly with severity did teach,
Each word of his authentic to allow,
That in the business there could be no breach,
Each thereto bound by a peculiar vow
  Which they in public generally protest,
  Calling the King to consummate the rest.

11.

Whose fair cheeks covered with pale sheets of
    shame,
Near in a swoon, he his first scene began,
Wherein his passions did such postures frame,
As every sense played the tragedian,
Truly to show from whence his sorrows came,
Far from the compass of a common man :
  As Nature to herself had added art,
  To teach Despair to act a kingly part.

12.

O Pity, didst thou live, or wert thou not?
Mortals by such sights have to stone been turned.
Or what men have been, had their seed forgot?
Or that for one another never mourned?
In what so strangely were ye over-shot,
Against yourselves, that your own frailty spurned?
   Or had tears then abandoned human eyes,
   That there was none to pity miseries?

13.

His passion calmed, his crown he taketh to him,
With a slight view, as though he thought not on it,
As he were senseless that it should forego him;
And then he casts a scornful eye upon it,
As he would leave it, yet would have it woo him;
Then snatching at it, loth to have foregone it,
   He puts it from him; yet he would not so,
   He fain would keep what fain he would forego.

14.

In this confuséd conflict in his mind,
Tears drowning sighs and sighs repelling tears;
But when in neither that he ease could find,
And to his wrong no remedy appears,
Perceiving none to pity there inclined,
Besides the time to him prefixéd wears;
   As then his sorrow somewhat 'gan to slake,
   From his full bosom thus he them bespake:

15.

"If first my title steadfastly were planted
Upon a true indubitate succession,
Confirmed by nations, as by Nature granted,
Which lawfully delivered me possession;
You must think Heaven sufficiency hath wanted,
And so deny it power by your oppression,
   That into question dare thus boldly bring
   The awful right of an anointed King.

16.

"That hallowed unction by a sacred hand,
Which once was poured upon this crownéd head,
And of this kingdom gave me the command
When it about me the rich verdure spread,
Either my right in greater stead should stand,
Or wherefore then was it so vainly shed?
   Whose profanation and unreverend touch,
   Just Heaven hath often punished, always much.

17.

"As from the sun, when from our sovereign due,
Whose virtual influence as the source of right
Lends safety of your livelihood to you,
As from our fulness taking borrowed light,
Which to the subject being ever true,
Why thus oppugn you by prepost'rous might?
   But what Heaven lent me wisely to have used,
   It gives to him that vainly I abused.

18.

"Then here I do resign it to your King."
Pausing thereat, as though his tongue offended,
With griping throes seemed forth that word to bring,
Sighing a full point as he there had ended.
O, how that sound his grievéd heart did wring!
Which he recalling gladly would have mended.
  Things of small moment we can scarcely hold,
  But griefs that touch the heart are hardly told.

19.

Which said, his eyes seemed to dissolve to tears,
After some great storm, like a shower of rain,
As his tongue strove to keep it from his ears,
Or he had spoke it with exceeding pain;
O, in his lips how vile that word appears,
Wishing it were within his breast again!
  Yet saith he, "Say so to the man you bear it,
  And thus say to him that you mean shall wear it:

20.

"Let him account his bondage from that day
That he was first with a diadem invested
(A goring crown hath made this hair so gray),
With that whose circle he is but arrested;
To true content this is no certain way,
With sweeter cates the mean estate is feasted:
  For when his proud feet scorn to touch the mould,
  His head's a prisoner in a gaol of gold.

21.

"In numbering subjects he but numbers care,
And when with shouts the people do begin,
Let him suppose the applause but prayers are,
That he may escape the danger he is in,
Wherein to adventure he so boldly dares :
The multitude hath multitudes of sin,
    And he that first doth cry, God save the King,
    Is the first man him evil news doth bring.

22.

"Lost in his own, misled in others' ways,
Soothed with deceits and fed with flatteries,
Himself displeasing wicked men to please,
Obeyed no more than he shall tyrannize,
The least in safety being most at ease,
With one friend winning many enemies ;
    And when he sitteth in his greatest state,
    They that behold him most, bear him most hate.

23.

"A King was he but now that now is none
Disarmed of power and here dejected is ;
By whose deposing he enjoys a throne
Who, were he natural, should not have done his :
I must confess the inheritance his own,
But whilst I live it should be none of his :
    But the son climbs and thrusts the father down,
    And thus the crownéd goes without a crown."

24.

Thus having played his hard constrainéd part,
His speech, his reign, the day together ended,
His breast shot through with sorrow's deadliest dart,
Cared for of none, nor looked on, unattended,
Sadly returning with a heavy heart
To his strait lodging strictly recommended,
    Left to bemoan his miserable plight
    To the deaf walls and to the darksome night.

25.

Whilst things were thus disastrously decreed,
Seditious libels every day were spread
By such as liked not of the violent deed,
That he by force should be deliveréd;
Whether his wrong remorse in some did breed,
That him, alas, untimely pitiéd,
    Who knew: or whether but devised by some
    To cloak his murder, afterward to come.

26.

And hate at hand, which hearkening still did lurk,
And still suspicious Edward was not sure,
Fearing that blood with Leicester might work,
Or that him friends his name might yet procure,
Which the Queen's faction mightily did irk,
At Kenilworth that no way could endure
    His longer stay, but cast to have him laid
    Where his friends least might hope to lend him aid.

27.

Of which, whenas they had debated long,
Of Berkeley Castle they themselves bethought,
A place by Nature that was wondrous strong,
And yet far stronger easily might be wrought:
Besides, it stood their chiefest friends among,
And where he was unlikeliest to be sought;
   And for their men to work what they desired,
   They knew where villains were that might be hired.

28.

For though the great, to cover their intent,
Seem not to know of any that are ill,
Yet want they not a devilish instrument,
Which they have ready ever at their will;
Such men these had, to mischief wholly bent,
In villany notorious for their skill,
   Dishonest, desperate, merciless, and rude,
   That dared into damnation to intrude.

29.

Vile Gurney and Maltravers were the men
Of this black scene the actors chose to be,
Whose hateful deed pollutes my maiden pen;
But, I beseech you, be not grieved with me,
Who have these names now, that were famous then;
Some boughs grow crooked from the straightest tree,
   Ye are no way partakers of their shame,
   The fault is in their fact, not in their name.

30.

To Kenilworth they speedily despatched,
Fitted with each thing that they could desire,
At such a time as few their coming watched,
When of their business none was to enquire ;
Well were the men and their commission matched,
For they had their authority entire,
   To take the King, his guardian to acquit,
   And to bestow him where they thought it fit.

31.

This crew of ribalds, villanous and nought,
With their co-agents in this damnéd thing,
To noble Leicester their commission brought,
Commanding the delivery of the King,
Which, with much grief, they lastly from him
    wrought,
About the castle closely hovering,
   Watching the time till silence and the night
   Could with convenience privilege their flight.

32.

With shameful scoffs and barbarous disgrace,
Him on a lean ill-favoured jade they set,
In a vile garment, beggarly and base,
Which it should seem they purposely did get ;
So carrying him in a most wretched case,
Benumbed and beaten with the cold and wet,
   Deprived of all repose and natural rest,
   With thirst and hunger grievously opprest.

33.

Yet still suspicious that he should be known,
From beard and head they shaved away the hair,
Which was the last that he could call his own;
Never left Fortune any wight so bare;
Such tyranny on King was never shown,
And, till that time, with mortals had been rare;
　　His comforts then did utterly deceive him,
　　But to his death his sorrows did not leave him.

34.

For when they had him far from all resort,
They took him down from his poor weary beast,
And on a molehill (for a state in Court)
With puddle water him they lewdly drest,
Then with his woful miseries made sport;
And for his basin, fitting with the rest,
　　A rusty iron skull; O wretched sight!
　　Was ever man so miserably dight?

35.

His tears increased the water with their fall,
Like a pool rising with a sudden rain,
Which wrestled with the puddle, and withal
A troubled circle made it to retain
His endless grief which to his mind did call,
His sighs made billows like a little main;
　　Water and tears contending whether should
　　The mastery have, the hot ones or the cold.

36.

Vile traitors, hold off your unhallowed hands,
His brow upon it majesty still bears ;
Dare ye thus keep your sovereign lord in bands?
And can your eyes behold the anointed's tears?
Or if your sight all pity thus withstands,
Are not your hearts yet pierc̀ed through your ears?
  The mind is free, whate'er afflict the man,
  A King's a King, do Fortune what she can.

37.

Dare man take that which God himself hath
    given?
Or mortal spill the spirit by him infused,
Whose power is subject to the power of Heaven?
Wrongs pass not unrevenged, although excused.
Except that thou set all at six and seven,
Rise, majesty, when thou art thus abused :
  Or for thy refuge which way wilt thou take,
  When in this sort thou dost thyself forsake?

38.

When in despite and mockery of a crown
A wreath of grass they for his temples make,
Which when he felt, then coming from a swoon,
And that his spirits a little 'gan to wake ;
"Fortune," quoth he, " thou dost not always frown,
I see thou giv'st as well as thou dost take,
  That wanting natural cover for my brain,
  For that defect thou lend'st me this again.

39.

"To whom, just Heaven, should I my grief
    complain,
Since it is only thou that workest all?
How can this body natural strength retain,
To suffer things so much unnatural?
My cogitations labour but in vain,
'Tis from thy justice that I have my fall,
   That when so many miseries do meet,
   The change of sorrow makes my torment sweet."

40.

Thus they to Berkeley brought the wretched King,
Which for their purpose was the place forethought.
Ye Heavenly Powers, do ye behold this thing
And let this deed of horror to be wrought,
That might the nation into question bring?
But O, your ways with justice still are fraught!
   But he is happed into his earthly hell,
   From whence he bade the wicked world farewell.

41.

They lodged him in a melancholy room,
Where through strait windows the dull light came far,
In which the sun did at no season come,
Which strengthened were with many an iron bar,
Like to a vault under some mighty tomb,
Where night and day waged a continual war;
   Under whose floor the common sewer past,
   Up to the same a loathsome stench that cast.

42.

The ominous raven often he doth hear,
Whose croaking him of following horror tells,
Begetting strange imaginary fear,
With heavy echoes, like to passing bells :
The howling dogs a doleful part doth bear,
As though they chimed his last sad burying knells :
　　Under his eave the buzzing screech-owl sings,
　　Beating the windows with her fatal wings.

43.

By night affrighted in his fearful dreams
Of raging fiends and goblins that he meets,
Of falling down from steep rocks into streams,
Of deaths, of burials, and of winding-sheets,
Of wandering helpless in far foreign realms,
Of strong temptations by seducing sprights ;
　　Wherewith awaked, and calling out for aid,
　　His hollow voice doth make himself afraid.

44.

Then came the vision of his bloody reign,
Marching along with Lancaster's stern ghost,
Twenty-eight Barons, either hanged or slain,
Attended with the rueful mangled host
That unrevenged did all that while remain,
At Burton Bridge, and fatal Borough lost ;
　　Threatening with frowns and quaking every limb,
　　As though that piecemeal they would torture him.

45.

And if it chanced that from the troubled skies
The least small star through any chink gave light,
Straightways on heaps the thronging clouds did rise,
As though that Heaven were angry with the night
That it should lend that comfort to his eyes;
Deforméd shadows glimpsing in his sight,
   As darkness, that it might more ugly be,
Through the least cranny would not let him see.

46.

When all the affliction that they could impose
Upon him, to the utmost of their hate,
Above his torments yet his strength so rose,
As though that Nature had conspired with Fate;
Whenas his watchful and too wary foes,
That ceased not still his woes to aggravate,
   His further helps suspected to prevent,
   To take away his life to Berkeley sent.

47.

And to that end a letter fashioning,
Which in the words a double sense did bear,
Which seemed to bid them not to kill the King,
Showing withal how vile a thing it were;
But by the pointing was another thing,
And to despatch him bids them not to fear:
   Which taught to find, the murderers need no more,
   Being thereto too ready long before.

48.

When Edward happed a chronicle to find
Of those nine Kings which did him there precede,
Which some there lodged forgotten had behind,
On which, to pass the hours, he fell to read,
Thinking thereby to recreate his mind ;
But in his breast that did sore conflicts breed :
    For when true sorrow once the fancy seizeth,
    Whate'er we see our misery increaseth.

49.

And to that Norman, entering on this isle,
Called William Conqueror, first his time he plies,
The fields of Hastings how he did defile
With Saxon blood, and Harold did surprise ;
And those which he so could not reconcile,
How over them he long did tyrannize :
    Where he read how the strong o'ercame the strong,
    As God ofttimes makes wrong to punish wrong.

50.

How Robert then, his eldest son, abroad,
Rufus, his second, seized on his estate,
His father's steps apparently that trode,
Depressing those who had been conquered late ;
But as on them he laid a heavy load,
So was he guerdoned by impartial fate :
    For whilst men's rooms for beasts he did intend,
    He in that Forest had a beastly end.

51.

Henry, his youngest, his brother William dead,
Taketh the crown from his usurping hand,
Due to the eldest, good Duke Robert's head,
Not then returnéd from the Holy Land;
Whose power was there so much diminishéd,
That he his foe not able to withstand,
　　Was ta'en in battle and his eyes outdone,
　　For which the seas left Henry not a son.

52.

To Maud the Empress he the sceptre leaves,
His only daughter, whom (through false pretext)
Stephen Earl of Boulogne from the kingdom heaves,
The Conqueror's nephew, in succession next,
By which the land a stranger war receives,
Wherewith it long was miserably vext:
　　Till Stephen failing and his issue gone,
　　The heir of Maud steps up into the throne.

53.

Henry the Second, Maud the Empress' son,
Of the English kings, Plantagenet the first,
By Stephen's end a glorious reign begun;
But yet his greatness strangely was accurst
By his son Henry's coronation:
Which to his age much woe and sorrow nurst,
　　When his, whom he had laboured to make great,
　　Abroad his towns, at home usurped his seat.

54.

Richard, his son, him worthily succeeds,
Who not content with what was safely ours,
(A man whose mind sought after glorious deeds)
Into the East transports the English powers ;
Where with his sword, whilst many a Pagan bleeds,
Relentless Fate doth haste on his last hours,
   By one whose sire he justly there had slain
   With a sharp arrow shot into the brain.

55.

Next followed him his faithless brother John,
By Arthur's murder, compassed by his might,
His brother Geoffrey, the Earl of Britain's son ;
But he by poison was repaid his spite ;
For whilst he strove to have made all his own,
For what he got by wrong he held his right,
   And on the clergy tyrannously fed,
   Was by a monk of Swinsted poisonéd.

56.

Henry his son, then crownéd very young,
For hate the English to the father bare,
The son's here reigning was in question long,
Who thought on France to have cast the kingdom's care ;
With whom the Barons, insolent and strong,
For the old Charter in commotion were :
   Which his long reign did with much care molest,
   Yet with much peace went lastly to his rest.

57.

Of him descends a Prince, stout, just, and sage
(In all things happy, but in him, his son),
In whom wise Nature did herself engage,
More than in man, in Edward to have done ;
Whose happy reign recurred the former rage,
By the large bounds he to his empire won :
  "O God," quoth he, "had he my pattern been,
  Heaven had not poured these plagues upon my sin!"

58.

Turning the leaf, he found at unawares
What day young Edward, Prince of Wales, was born ;
Which letters looked like conjuring characters,
Or to despite him they were set in scorn,
Blotting the paper like disfiguring scars :
"O, let that name," quoth he, "from books be torn,
  Lest in that place the sad displeaséd earth
  Doth loathe itself, as slandered with my birth.

59.

"Be thence hereafter human birth exiled,
Sunk to a lake, or swallowed by the sea ;
And future ages, asking for that child,
Say 'twas abortive, or 'twas stolen away ;
And lest, O Time, thou be therewith defiled,
In thy unnumbered hours devour that day :
  Let all be done that power can bring to pass,
  To make forgot that such a one there was."

60.

The troubled tears then standing in his eyes,
Through which he did upon the letters look,
Made them to seem like roundlets that arise
By a stone cast into a standing brook,
Appearing to him in such various wise,
And at one time such sundry fashions took,
　　As like deluding goblins did affright,
　　And with their foul shapes terrify his sight.

61.

And on his deathbed sits him down at last,
His fainting spirits foreshowing danger nigh,
When the doors forth a fearful howling cast,
To let those in by whom he was to die;
At whose approach, whilst there he lay aghast,
Those ruthless villains did upon him fly:
　　Who, seeing none to whom to call for aid,
　　Thus to these cruel regicides he said:

62.

"O be not authors of so vile an act,
My blood on your posterity to bring,
Which after-time with horror shall distract,
When fame shall tell it how you killed a King;
And yet more, by the manner of the fact,
Mortality so much astonishing,
　　That they should count their wickedness scarce sin,
　　Compared to that which done by you hath been.

63.

"And since you deadly hate me, let me live;
Yea, this advantage angry Heaven hath left,
Which, except life, hath ta'en what it did give;
But that revenge should not from you be reft,
Me yet with greater misery to grieve,
Hath still reserved this from its former theft;
   That this, which might of all these plagues prevent me,
   Were I deprived it, lasteth to torment me."

64.

Thus spake this woful and distresséd lord,
As yet his breath found passage to and fro,
With many a short pant, many a broken word,
Many a sore groan, many a grievous throe,
Whilst him his spirit could any strength afford
To his last gasp, to move them with his woe;
   Till overmastered by their too much strength,
   His sickly heart submitted at the length.

65.

When 'twixt two beds they closed his wearied corse,
Basely uncovering his most secret part,
And without human pity or remorse,
With a hot spit they thrust him to the heart.
O that my pen had in it but that force
To express the pain! but that surpasseth art;
   And that the soul must even with trembling do,
   For words want weight, nor can they reach thereto.

66.

When those (i' th' depth and dead time of the night)
Poor simple people, that then dwellèd near,
Whom that strange noise did wondrously affright,
That his last shriek did in his parting hear,
As pitying that most miserable wight,
(Betwixt compassion and obedient fear)
　　Turned up their eyes, with heaviness opprest,
　　Praying to Heaven to give the soul good rest.

67.

Berkeley, whose fair seat hath been famous long,
Let thy sad echoes shriek a deadly sound,
To the vast air complain his grievous wrong,
And keep the blood that issued from his wound,
The tears that dropped from his dead eyes among,
In their black footsteps printed on the ground,
　　Thereby that all the ages that succeed
　　May call to mind the foulness of their deed.

68.

Let thy large buildings still retain his groans,
His sad complaints by learning to repeat,
And let the dull walls and the senseless stones
By the impression of his torment sweat,
And for not able to express his moans,
Therefore with pain and agony replete,
　　That all may thither come that shall be told it,
　　As in a mirror clearly to behold it.

E

69.

And let the Genius of that woful place
Become the guide to his more frightful ghost,
With hair dishevelled and a ghastly face,
And haunt the prison where his life was lost,
And as the den of horror and disgrace,
Let it be fearful over all the coast;
   That those hereafter that do travel near
   Never may view it but with heavy cheer.

THE SIXTH CANTO.

THE ARGUMENT.

Lord Mortimer made Earl of March, how he
And the bright Queen rule all things by their might;
The state wherein at Nottingham they be,
The cost wherewith their pompous Court is dight,
Envied by those their hateful pride that see:
The King attempts the dreadful cave by night,
   Entering the Castle, taketh him from thence,
   And March at London dies for his offence.

1.

Now, whilst of sundry accidents we sing,
Some of much sadness, others of delight,
In our conceit strange objects fashioning;
We our free numbers tenderly invite
Somewhat to slack this melancholy string:
For we too soon of death come to indite,
   When things of moment in the course we hold
   Fall in their order fitly to be told.

2.

Whilst they the hours do carefully redeem,
Their fraudful courses finely to contrive,
How foul soe'er, to make them fair to seem,
For which they all did diligently strive,
To tempt men still so of them to esteem
That all might wish their purposes to thrive :
   For it was cunning mixéd with their might,
   That had and still must make their wrong seem right.

3.

The pompous Synod of those earthly gods
Was then assigned to Salisbury, to bring
Things to be even that had been at odds,
To the fair entrance of the new-crowned King,
And thereby so to settle their abodes
That peace from their first Parliament might spring :
   Wisely to end what well they had begun,
   For many thought that strange things had been done.

4.

Whilst Mortimer (so lord of his desire
That none prevailed his purpose to defeat)
His style of Baron heaved an Earldom higher,
To extend the honour of his ancient seat,
That his command might be the more entire ;
Who only then but the Earl of March was great?
   Who knew the land into her lap was thrown,
   Which having all would never starve her own.

5.

And firm they stood, as those two steadfast poles
'Twixt which this all doth on the axtree move,
Whose strength the frame of government upholds,
Which to those times their wisdoms did approve:
Strong must that fate be which their will controls,
Or had the power them from their seats to shove:
    For well they found that that which they could feel
    Must of force make the realm itself to reel.

6.

When Edward's nonage, that of peace had need,
The Scot encouraged to renew the war,
Of which it much behoved them to take heed,
Matters so strangely managed as they were,
Which should they suffer by neglect to breed
Nothing they yet had made but it might mar,
    Which for their good, reserving their estate,
    They prove to purchase at the dearest rate.

7.

Nor less than Ragman the rough Scot sufficed,
Of all our writings of the most renown,
By which the Kings of Scotland had demised
Their yearly homage to the English Crown,
With other relics that were highly prized,
But that which made the patient'st men to frown
    Was the black Cross of Scotland, ominous deemed
    Before all other anciently esteemed.

8.

To colour which and to confirm the peace,
They made a marriage between them and us,
And for a strong pretext to that release,
Which to the wisest seemed most dangerous,
Whilst Robert reigned, and after his decease
That it might last, it was concluded thus:
　　David their Prince our Princess Joan should take,
　　Betwixt the realms a lasting league to make.

9.

When the Earl of Kent, that had been long of
　　those
Which in their actions had a powerful hand,
Perceiving them of matters to dispose
Tending to the subversion of the land,
And further danger daily did disclose,
If that the kingdom they should still command;
　　Whilst he their fall did cunningly forecast,
　　Did but his own too violently haste.

10.

For giving out his brother to survive,
Of all men calléd the deceaséd King,
Into the people's head such doubts did drive
As into question Edward's right did bring.
Ill this report was raised, and worse did thrive,
Being so foul and dangerous a thing;
　　That as a mover of intestine strife
　　He for the treason forfeited his life.

11.

Whilst Edward takes but what they only give,
Whose nonage craved their carefullest protection,
Who knew to rule, and he but learned to live,
From their experience taking his direction:
Hard was the thing that they could not contrive,
When he that reigned was crowned by their election;
   And that the right which did to him belong,
   And must uphold him, chiefly made them strong.

12.

Providing for the council of the King
Those of most power, the noblest of the Peers,
Experienced well, complete in everything,
Whose judgments had been ripened with their years,
With comeliness their actions managing:
Yet whilst they row 'tis Mortimer that steers;
   Well might we think the man were more than blind
   That wanted sea-room and could rule the wind.

13.

Keeping their course that it still clearly shone,
By the most curious cunning to be scanned,
And make that which was Edward's then their own,
Being received from his sovereign hand,
Into their bosoms absolutely thrown
Both for his good and safety of his land,
   All their proceedings coloured with that care
   To the world's eye so fair an outside bare.

14.

And they which could the complements of State
To greatness gave each ceremonious rite,
To their designs to give the longer date,
The like again in others to excite;
In entertaining love they welcomed hate,
And to one banquet freely both invite;
  A Prince's wealth by spending still doth spread,
  Like to a brook by many fountains fed.

15.

To Nottingham the North's imperious eye,
Which as a Pharus doth survey the soil,
Arméd by Nature danger to defy;
March, to repose him after all his toil,
Where treason least advantage might espy,
Closely conveyed his past-price valued spoil;
  That there residing from the public sight
  He might with pleasure relish his delight.

16.

Ninescore in check belonging to their Court,
By honoured knighthood knit in mutual bands,
Men most select, of special worth and sort;
Much might they do that had so many hands;
March and the Queen maintain one equal port
In that proud castle which so far commands;
  From whence they seémed as they like those would
    rise
  Who once threw rocks at the imperial skies.

17.

As Fortune meant her power on March to show,
And in her arms to bear him through the sky,
By him to daunt whosoever sat below,
Having above them mounted him so high :
Who at his beck was he that did not bow,
If at his feet he did not humbly lie ?
　　All things concur with more than happy chance
　　To raise the man whom Fortune will advance.

18.

Here all along the flower-befilléd vales
On her clear lands the silver Trent doth slide,
And to the meadows, telling wanton tales,
Her crystal limbs lasciviously, in pride,
As ravishéd with the enamoured gales,
With often turnings casts from side to side ;
　　As she were loth the fair sight to forsake
　　And run herself into the German lake.

19.

And North from thence, rude Sherwood as she roves
Casts many a long look at those lofty towers,
And with the thickness of her well-grown groves,
Shelters the town from stormy winter's showers,
In pleasant summer, and to show her loves,
Bids it again to see her shady bowers :
　　Courting the castle which, as turning to her,
　　Smiles to behold the enamoured wood-nymph woo her.

20.

March and the Queen so planted in that place,
Thither in person princely Edward draws,
Who seemed their friendships friendly to embrace
And upon every little offered cause
Ready to do them ceremonious grace ;
Whom they observe, of Court that knew the laws ;
    Whilst in the town King Edward took his seat,
    The Queen's great confluence made the castle sweat.

21.

Where, when they pleased in council to debate,
Or they the King at any pleasure met,
They came with such magnificence of state
As did all eyes upon their greatness set,
Prizing their presence at that costly rate
As to the same due reverence might beget ;
    Which in most people admiration wrought,
    And much amazéd many a wandering thought.

22.

O, could ambition apprehend a stay,
The giddy course it wandereth in to guide !
And give it safety in that slippery way
Where the most worldly provident do slide,
It not so soon should see its own decay ;
But it so much besotted is with pride
    That it ne'er thinketh of that pit at all
    Wherein, through boldness, it doth blindly fall.

23.

But never doth it surfeit with excess,
Each dish so savoury, seasoned with delight,
Nor nothing can the gluttony suppress,
But still it longs, so liquorish is the sight,
Nor having all is in desire the less,
Till it so much be tempted past the might,
　　That the full stomach, more than well sufficed,
　　Vomits what late it vilely gormandized.

24.

Like to some low brook from a loftier ground
By waste of waters that is overflowed,
Is sated, till it shouldereth down the mound,
And the old course quite of itself unload,
That where it was it after is not found,
But from the strait banks lays itself abroad,
　　Leading the fountain that doth feed it by
　　So leaves the channel desolate and dry.

25.

Whenas those few that many tears had spent,
By gazing long on murdered Edward's grave,
Muttered in corners, grieved and discontent;
And finding those them willing ear that gave,
Still as they durst discovered what they meant,
Tending their pride and greatness to deprave;
　　Urging withal what some might justly do,
　　If things so borne were rightly looked into.

26.

And some gave out, that Mortimer to rise
Had cut off Kent, that next was to succeed,
Whose treasons they avowed March to surmise,
As a mere colour to that lawless deed ;
Which his ambition only did devise
Quite out the Royal Family to weed,
    And made account, if Edward once were gone,
    He o'er the rest might step into the throne.

27.

As those his favourers, in those former times,
Then credulous that honour was his end,
And for the hate they bare to others' crimes
Did not his faults so carefully attend:
Perceiving he so dissolutely climbs,
Having then brought his purpose to an end,
    With a severe eye did more strictly look
    Into the course which his ambition took.

28.

All fence the tree that serveth for a shade,
Whose big-grown body doth bear off the wind,
Till that his wasteful branches do invade
The new-sprung plants, and them in prison bind ;
Whenas a tyrant to his weaker made,
And as a vile devourer of his kind,
    All lend their hands at his large root to hew
    Whose greatness hindereth others that would grow.

29.

So at his ease securely whilst he sate,
And as he would so all things settled were,
Under the guidance of a gracious fate,
Never more free from jealousy and fear;
So great his mind, so mighty his estate,
As they admit not danger to be near:
   But still we see, before a sudden shower,
   The sun upon us hath the greatest power.

30.

Within the castle had the Queen devised,
Long about which she busied had her thought,
A chamber, wherein she imparadised
What shapes for her could anywhere be sought;
Which in the same were curiously comprised
By skilful painters, excellently wrought:
   And in the place of greatest safety there,
   Which she had named the Tower of Mortimer.

31.

A room prepared with pilasters she chose,
That to the roof their slender points did rear,
Arching the top, whereas they all did close,
Which from below showed like an hemisphere;
In whose concavity she did compose
The constellations that to us appear
   In their corporeal shapes, with stars enchased,
   As by the old poets they on Heaven were placed.

32.

About which lodging, towards the upper face,
Ran a fine border, circularly led,
As equal 'twixt the zenith and the base,
Which as a zone the waist engirdlèd,
That lent the sight a breathing, by the space
'Twixt things near hand and those far overhead,
  Upon the plain wall of which lower part
  Painting expressed the utmost of her art.

33.

There Phœbus clipping Hyacinthus stood,
Whose life's last drops did the god's breast imbrue,
His tears so mixèd with the young boy's blood,
That whether was the more no eye could view;
And though together lost as in a flood,
Yet here and there the one from the other drew:
  The pretty wood-nymphs chasing him with balm,
  Proving to wake him from his deadly qualm.

34.

Apollo's quiver and far-killing bow,
His gold-fringed mantle on the grassful grouna,
To express whose act, Art even her best did show,
The sledge so shadowed still as to rebound,
As it had scarce done giving of the blow,
Lending a lasting freshness to the wound;
  The purple flower from the boy's blood begun,
  That since ne'er spreads but to the rising sun.

35.

Near that was Iö in a heifer's shape,
Viewing her new-ta'en figure in a brook,
In which her shadow seemed on her to gape
As on the same she greedily did look,
To see how Jove could cloud his wanton 'scape;
So done that the beholders oft mistook
    Themselves; to some that one way did allow
    A woman's likeness, the other way a cow.

36.

There Mercury was like a shepherd's boy,
Sporting with Hebe by a fountain brim,
With many a sweet glance, many an amorous toy;
He sprinkling drops at her, and she at him:
Wherein the painter so explained their joy
As he had meant the very life to limn:
    For on their brows he made the drops so clear
    That through each drop their fair skins did appear.

37.

By them in landscape rocky Cynthus reared,
With the clouds leaning on his lofty crown,
On his sides showing many a straggling herd,
And from his top the clear springs creeping down
By the old rocks, each with a hoary beard,
With moss and climbing ivy overgrown:
    So done that the beholders with the skill
    Never enough their longing eyes could fill.

38.

The half-naked nymphs, some climbing, some descending,
The sundry flowers at one another flung,
In postures strange their limber bodies bending ;
Some cropping branches that seemed lately sprung,
Upon the brakes their coloured mantles rending,
Which on the mount grew here and there among ;
  Combing their hair some, some made garlands by,
  So strove the painter to content the eye.

39.

In one part, Phaëton cast amongst the clouds
By Phœbus' palfreys, that their reins had broke,
His chariot tumbling from the welkéd shrouds,
And the fierce steeds flew madding from their yoke,
The elements confusedly in crowds,
And heaven and earth were nought but flame and smoke ;
  A piece so done that many did desire
  To warm themselves, some frighted with the fire ;

40.

And into Padus falling, as he burned,
Thereinto thrown by Jove out of the skies ;
His weeping sisters there to trees were turned,
Yet so of women did retain the guise,
That none could censure, whether as they mourned
Drops from their boughs, or tears fell from their eyes ;
  Done for the last, with such exceeding life,
  As Art therein with Nature seemed at strife.

41.

And for the light to this brave lodging lent,
The workman, who as wisely could direct,
Did for the same the windows so invent
That they should artificially reflect
The day alike on every lineament
To their proportion, and had such respect
 As that the beams, condensated and grave,
 To every figure a sure colour gave.

42.

In part of which, under a golden vine,
Which held a curious canopy through all,
Stood a rich bed, quite covered with the twine,
Shadowing the same in the redoubling fall,
Whose clusters drew the branches to decline,
'Mongst which did many a naked Cupid sprawl:
 Some at the sundry-coloured birds did shoot,
 And some, about to pluck the purple fruit.

43.

On which a tissue counterpane was cast,
Arachne's web did not the same surpass,
Wherein the story of his fortunes past
In lively pictures neatly handled was,
How he escaped the Tower, in France how graced,
With stones embroidered of a wondrous mass;
 About the border, in a fine-wrought fret,
 Emblems, impresses, hieroglyphics set.

44.

This flattering sunshine had begot the shower,
And the black clouds with such abundance fed,
That for a wind they waited but the hour
With force to let their fury on his head ;
Which when it came, it came with such a power
As he could hardly have imagined :
　　But when men think they most in safety stand,
　　Their greatest peril often is at hand.

45.

For to that largeness they increaséd were,
That Edward felt March heavy on his throne,
Whose props no longer both of them could bear,
Two for one seat that over-great were grown,
Preposterously that movéd in one sphere,
And to the like predominancy prone,
　　That the young King down Mortimer must cast,
　　If he himself would e'er hope to sit fast.

46.

Who finding the necessity was such
That urged him still the assault to undertake,
And yet his person it might nearly touch
Should he too soon his sleeping power awake ;
The attempt, wherein the danger was so much,
Drove him at length a secret means to make
　　Whereby he might the enterprise effect,
　　And hurt him most where he did least suspect.

47.

Without the castle, in the earth is found
A cave, resembling sleepy Morpheus' cell,
In strange meanders winding underground,
Where darkness seeks continually to dwell,
Which with such fear and horror doth abound
As though it were an entrance into hell:
   By architects to serve the castle, made
   Whenas the Danes this island did invade.

48.

Now, on along the crankling path doth keep,
Then by a rock turns up another way,
Rising towards day, then falling towards the deep,
On a smooth level then itself doth lay,
Directly then, then obliquely doth creep,
Nor in the course keeps any certain stay,
   Till in the castle, in an odd by-place,
   It casts the foul mask from its dusky face.

49.

By which the King, with a selected crew
Of such as he with his intent acquainted,
Which he affected to the action knew,
And in revenge of Edward had not fainted,
That to their utmost would the cause pursue,
And with those treasons that had not been tainted,
   Adventuréd the labyrinth to essay,
   To rouse the beast which kept them all at bay.

50.

Long after Phœbus took his labouring team
To his pale sister and resigned his place,
To wash his cauples in the ocean stream,
And cool the fervour of his glowing face;
And Phœbe, scanted of her brother's beam,
Into the West went after him apace,
  Leaving black darkness to possess the sky,
  To fit the time of that black tragedy.

51.

What time by torchlight they attempt the cave,
Which at their entrance seeméd in a fright
With the reflection that their armour gave,
As it till then had ne'er seen any light;
Which striving there pre-eminence to have,
Darkness therewith so daringly doth fight
  That each confounding other, both appear
  As darkness light, and light but darkness were.

52.

The craggy cleeves which cross them as they go,
Made as their passage they would have denied,
And threatened them their journey to foreslow,
As angry with the path that was their guide,
And sadly seemed their discontent to show
To the vile hand that did them first divide:
  Whose cumbrous falls and risings seemed to say
  So ill an action could not brook the day.

53.

And by the lights as they along were led,
Their shadows then them following at their back,
Were like to mourners carrying forth their dead,
And as the deed so were they ugly black,
Or like to fiends that them had followéd,
Pricking them on to bloodshed and to wrack;
　Whilst the light looked as it had been amazed
　At their deforméd shapes whereon it gazed.

54.

The clattering arms their masters seemed to chide,
As they would reason wherefore they should wound,
And struck the cave in passing on each side,
As they were angry with the hollow ground
That it an act so pitiless should hide ;
Whose stony roof locked in their angry sound,
　And hanging in the creeks, drew back again,
　As willing them from murder to refrain.

55.

The night waxed old (not dreaming of these
　　things),
And to her chamber is the Queen withdrawn,
To whom a choice musician plays and sings
Whilst she sat under an estate of lawn,
In night attire more godlike glittering
Than any eye had seen the cheerful dawn,
　Leaning upon her most loved Mortimer,
　Whose voice, more than the music, pleased her ear.

56.

Where her fair breasts at liberty were let,
Whose violet veins in branchéd riverets flow,
And Venus' swans and milky doves were set
Upon those swelling mounts of driven snow ;
Whereon, whilst Love to sport himself doth get,
He lost his way, nor back again could go,
  But with those banks of beauty set about
  He wandered still, yet never could get out.

57.

Her loose hair looked like gold (O word too base !
Nay, more than sin but so to name her hair)
Declining, as to kiss her fairer face,
No word is fair enough for thing so fair,
Nor ever was there epithet could grace
That by much praising which we much impair ;
  And where the pen fails, pencils cannot show it,
  Only the soul may be supposed to know it.

58.

She laid her fingers on his manly cheek,
The god's pure sceptres and the darts of love,
That with their touch might make a tiger meek
Or might great Atlas from his seat remove ;
So white, so soft, so delicate, so sleek,
As she had worn a lily for a glove,
  As might beget life where was never none,
  And put a spirit into the hardest stone.

59.

The fire, of precious wood ; the light perfume,
Which left a sweetness on each thing it shone,
As everything did to itself assume
The scent from them, and made the same their own :
So that the painted flowers within the room
Were sweet, as if they naturally had grown ;
   The light gave colours which upon them fell,
   And to the colours the perfume gave smell.

60.

When on those sundry pictures they devise,
And from one piece they to another run,
Commend that face, that arm, that hand, those eyes,
Show how that bird, how well that flower was done,
How this part shadowed, and how that did rise,
This top was clouded, how that trail was spun,
   The landscape, mixture, and delineatings,
   And in that art a thousand curious things.

61.

Looking upon proud Phaëton wrapped in fire,
The gentle Queen did much bewail his fall ;
But Mortimer commended his desire,
To lose one poor life or to govern all :
"What though," quoth he "he madly did aspire,
And his great mind made him proud Fortune's thrall ?
   Yet in despite, when she her worst had done,
   He perished in the chariot of the sun."

62.

"Phœbus," she said, "was over-forced by Art,"
Nor could she find how that embrace could be:
But Mortimer then took the painter's part,
"Why thus, bright Empress, thus and thus," quoth he;
"That hand doth hold his back, and this his heart,
Thus their arms twine, and thus their lips, you see;
  Now are you Phœbus, Hyacinthus I,
  It were a life thus every hour to die."

63.

When by that time into the Castle hall
Was rudely entered that well-arméd rout,
And they within suspecting nought at all,
Had then no guard to watch for them without:
See how mischances suddenly do fall,
And steal upon us, being farth'st from doubt:
  Our life's uncertain and our death is sure,
  And towards most peril man is most secure.

64.

Whilst youthful Nevil and brave Turrington,
To the bright Queen that ever waited near,
Two with great March much credit that had won,
That in the lobby with the ladies were,
Staying delight, whilst time away did run,
With such discourse as women love to hear;
  Charged on the sudden by the arméd train,
  Were at their entrance miserably slain.

65.

When, as from snow-crowned Skiddaw's lofty cleeves
Some fleet-winged haggard, towards her preying hour,
Amongst the teal and moor-bred mallard drives
And the air of all her feathered flock doth scour,
Whilst to regain her former height she strives,
The fearful fowl all prostrate to her power:
    Such a sharp shriek did ring throughout the vault,
    Made by the women at the fierce assault.

66.

Unarmed was March (she only in his arms,
Too soft a shield to bear their boist'rous blows),
Who least of all suspected such alarms,
And to be so encountered by his foes,
When he was most improvident of harms.
O, had he had but weapons to his woes!
    Either his valour had his life redeemed,
    Or in her sight died happily esteemed.

67.

But there, about him looking for the King,
Whom he supposed his judgment could not miss;
Which when he found by his imagining
Of those most perfect lineaments of his:
Quoth he, "The man that to thy crown did bring
Thee, at thy hands might least have looked for this;
    And in this place the least of all the rest,
    Where only sacred solitude is blest.

68.

"Her presence frees the offender of this ill,
Whose godlike greatness makes the place divine ;
And canst thou, King, thus countermand her will
Who gave to thee the power that now is thine,
And in her arms in safety kept thee still,
As in a most inviolated shrine?
   Yet darest thou irreligiously despise,
   And thus profane, these sacred liberties."

69.

But even as when old Ilion was surprised
The Grecians issuing from the wooden horse,
The pride and fury roughly exercised,
Opening the wide gates, letting in their force,
Putting in act what was before devised,
Without all human pity or remorse ;
   Even so did they with whose confuséd sound
   Words were not heard, and poor complaints were
      drowned.

70.

Dissolved to tears, she followed him : O tears !
Elixir-like, turn all to pearl you touch ;
To weep with her the hard wall scarce forbears,
The woful words she utteréd were such
Able to wound the impenetrablest ears,
Her plaints so piercing and her grief so much :
   And to the King when she at last could come,
   Thus to him spake, though he to her were dumb.

71.

"Dear son," quoth she, "let not his blood be spilt,
So often ventured to redeem thy crown,
In all his life can there be found that guilt?
Think of his love, on which thou once shouldst frown:
'Twas he thy seat that so substantial built,
Long with his shoulder saved from shaking down;
  'Twas he the means that first for thee did find
  To pass for France to exercise thy mind.

72.

"Even for the love thou bear'st to that dear blood
From which, my son, thou didst receive thy life,
Play not the niggard in so small a good
With her to whom thy bounties should be rife,
Begged on those knees at which thou oft hast stood;
O, let my upheld hands appease this strife!
  Let not the breath from this sad bosom sent,
  Without thy pity be but vainly spent."

73.

When in the tumult, with the sudden fright,
Whilst every one for safety sought about,
And none regarded to maintain the light,
Which being over-wasted was gone out,
It being then the midtime of the night
Ere they could quit the castle of the rout;
  The Queen alone—at least if any near
  They were her women, almost dead with fear.

74.

When horror, darkness, and her inward woe
Began to work on her afflicted mind,
Upon her weakness tyrannizing so
As they would do their utmost in their kind,
And as than those she need no other foe,
Such power her fortune had to them assigned
  To rack her conscience by their torture due,
  Itself to accuse of whatsoe'er it knew.

75.

"O God!" thought she, "is yet an hour scarce past,
Since that my greatness, my command more high,
And eminency, wherein I was placed,
Won me respect in every humble eye?
How am I now abuséd? how disgraced?
Did ever Queen in my dejection lie?"
  These things she pondered as despair still brought
  Their sundry forms into her troubled thought.

76.

To London thus they March a prisoner led,
Which there had oft been courted by the Queen,
From whom his friends and his late followers fled,
Of many a gallant followed that had been
Of which there was not one durst show his head,
Much less to abet his side that durst be seen;
  Which at his fall made them to wonder more
  Who saw the pomp wherein he lived before.

77.

O misery! where once thou art possest,
See but how quickly thou canst alter kind,
And like a Circe metamorphosest
The man that hath not a most godlike mind :
The fainting spirit, O how thou canst infest!
Whose yielding frailty easily thou canst find,
    And by thy vicious presence with a breath
    Gives him up fettered, basely feared, to death.

78.

When soon the King a Parliament decreed,
Ne'er till that time sole master of his crown,
And against March doth legally proceed,
Fitted with tools to dig that mountain down,
To which both high and low took special heed ;
He ne'er had fawn, but then he had a frown,
    King Edward's blood, with both the Spensers', call
    For vengeance on him, by the voice of all.

79.

With dear Kent's death his credit next they blot,
Then on him lay the wards and liveries
Which he by craft into his hands had got,
The sums then seizéd to his treasuries ;
Then Joan the Princess, married to the Scot,
The sign at Stanhope to the enemies ;
    With all things ripped from the recórds of time
    That any way might aggravate his crime.

80.

O dire revenge! when thou by time art raked
Out of the ashes which have hid thee long,
(Wherein thou layest as thou hadst quite been slaked)
And becom'st kindled with the breath of wrong,
How soon thy hideous fury is awaked?
From thy poor sparks what flames are quickly sprung?
  To waste their tops how soon dost thou aspire
  Whose weight and greatness once represt thy fire?

81.

And what availed his answer in that case?
Which the time then did utterly distaste,
And looked upon him with so stern a face
As it his actions utterly disgraced;
No friendly bosom gave him any place
Who was clean out of all opinion cast;
  Taking his pen, his sorrows to deceive,
  Thus of the Queen he lastly took his leave.

82.

"Bright Empress, yet be pleaséd to peruse
The swan-like dirges of a dying man,
Although not like the raptures of the Muse
In our fresh youth, when our love first began,
Into my breast that did the fire infuse
That glorious day that I thy rich glove won,
  And in my course a flame of lightning bet
  Out of proud Hertford's high-plumed burgonet.

83.

"As for your son, that hasteneth on my death,
Madam, you know I loved him as mine own,
And when I could have graspéd out his breath,
I set him easily on his father's throne ;
Which now his power too quickly witnesseth,
Who to this height in tyranny is grown ;
　　But yet be his ingratitude forgiven,
　　As, after death, I wish to be in heaven.

84.

"And for the sole rule whereon so he stands
Came bastard William but himself to shore?
Or had he not our father's valiant hands,
Who in that field our ancient ensign bore.
(Guarded about with our well-ordered bands)
Which then his leopards for their safety wore,
　　Looking at Hastings like that ominous lake
　　From whose black depths our glorious name we take?

85.

"Why fell I not from that my all-armed horse,
On which I rode before the gates of Gaunt,
Before the Belgic and Burgonian force,
There challenging their countries' combatant;
Cast from my feet in some robustious course,
That they of me the victory might vaunt?
　　Why sunk I not under my battered shield,
　　To grace a brave foe and renown a field?

86.

"Yet never servèd I Fortune like a slave,
Nor have, through baseness, made her bounties less,
In me her judgment poorly to deprave,
Nought hath she lent me that I'll not confess:
Nay, interest for her principal I gave,
My mind hath suited with her mightiness,
   Her frowns with scorn and Mortimer doth bear
   For nothing can she do that he can fear.

87.

"That ne'er quails me at which your greatest quake,
Nor aught that's dreadful danger me can show,
Through sword and fire so used my way to take:
In death what can be that I do not know,
That I should fear a covenant to make
With it, which welcomed, finisheth my woe?
   And nothing can the afflicted conscience grieve,
   But He may pardon who can all forgive.

88.

"And thus, thou most adorèd in my heart,
The thoughts of whom my humbled spirit doth raise,
Lady most fair, most dear, of most desert,
Worthy of more than any mortal praise,
Condemnèd March thus lastly doth depart
From the great'st Empress living in her days;
   Nor with my dust mine honour I inter:
   Cæsar thus died, and thus dies Mortimer."

89.

When secretly he sent this letter to her,
Whose supersciption was her princely style,
She knew the hand, and thought it came to woo her,
With which conceit she pleased herself a while,
Than which no one thing served so to undo her,
By feeding her with flattery and with guile
   To make her still more sensible of pain
   Which her sad heart was shortly to sustain.

90.

Using her fingers to rip up the seal
Which helped to hide these ill news from her eyes,
Loth as it were such tidings to reveal
As might her senses suddenly surprise;
But when her white hand did so hardly deal
With the poor paper that the wax must rise,
   It stuck upon her fingers bloody red,
   As to portend some dear blood should be shed.

91.

When by degrees she easily doth begin,
And as a fish plays with a baited hook,
So softly yet she swallowed sorrow in,
Till she her bane into her bowels took;
And then she sees the expenses of her sin,
Sadly set down in that black doomsday book,
   And the dear sums that were to be defrayed
   Before the debt were absolutely paid.

92.

Whole hosts of sorrows her sick heart assail,
When every letter lanced her like a dart,
Striving against her which should most prevail,
And yet not one but pricked her to the heart;
Where one word might another's woe bewail,
And with its neighbour seemed to bear a part,
    Each line served for so true a text to her,
    As in her woes would no way let her err.

93.

Grief bade her look, yet soon it bade her leave,
Wherewith o'ercharged she neither sees nor hears,
Her usefullest senses soonest her deceive,
The sight shuts up her eyes, the sound her ears,
And of her reading doth her quite bereave,
When for a fescue she doth use her tears,
    Which when some line she loosely overpast
    The drops could tell her where she left the last.

94.

Somewhat at length recovering of her sight,
Deeply she cursed her sorrow-seeing eye,
And said she was deluded by the light,
Or was abused by the orthography,
Or some one had devisèd it in spite,
Pointing it false, her scholarship to try:
    Thus when we fondly flatter our desires,
    Our best conceits do prove the greatest liars.

F

95.

Her trembling hand as in a fever quakes,
Wherewith the paper doth a little stir,
Which she imagines at her sorrow shakes,
And pities it which she think pities her;
Each small thing somewhat to the greater makes,
And to her humour something doth infer:
　　Her woe-tied tongue but when she once could free,
　　" Sweet Mortimer, my most loved lord," quoth she,

96.

" For thy dear ashes be my breast the urn,
Which as a relic I of thee will save,
Mixed with the tears that I for thee shall mourn,
Which in this bosom shall their burial have;
Out of which place they never shall return,
Nor give the honour to another grave:
　　But here, as in a temple, be preserved,
　　Wherein thy image is most lively carved."

97.

Then breaks she out in cursing of her son,
But Mortimer so runneth in her mind
As that she ended ere she had begun,
Speaking before what should have come behind;
From that she to another course doth run,
To be revenged in some notorious kind:
　　By stab, or poison, and she'll swear to both,
　　But for her life she could not find an oath.

98.

She pen and paper takes, and makes no doubt
But the King's cruel dealing to discover;
But soon forgetting what she went about,
Poor Queen, she fell to scribbling to her lover;
Here she put in, and there she blotted out;
Her passion did so violently move her,
    That turning back to read what she had writ,
    She tore the paper and condemned her wit.

99.

But from her passion being somewhat raised,
Like one that lately had been in a swound
Or felt some strange extremity appeased
That had been taken from some blow or wound,
Yet on that part it had so strongly seized,
That for the same no remedy was found:
    But at the very point their life to lose,
    As they their goods, she doth her grief dispose.

100.

Quoth she, "King Edward, as thou art my son,
Leaving the world, this legacy I leave thee:
My heart's true love my Mortimer hath won,
And yet of all he shall not so bereave thee;
But for this mischief to thy mother done,
Take thou my curse, so that it may outlive thee,
    That as thy deed doth daily me torment,
    So may my Curse thee, by my testament.

101.

"And henceforth in this solitary place,
Ever residing from the public sight,
A private life I willingly embrace,
No more rejoicing in the obvious light,
To consummate this too long lingering space,
Till death enclose me in continual night,
    Let never sleep more close my wearied eye,
    So, Isabella, lay thee down and die."

HEROICAL EPISTLES.

QUEEN ISABEL TO MORTIMER.

THE ARGUMENT.

Fair Isabel, Edward the Second's Queen,
Philip of France his daughter, for the spleen
She bare her husband, for that he affected
Lascivious minions and her love neglected,
Drew to her favour, striving to prefer,
That valiant young Lord Roger Mortimer:
Who with the Barons rose, but wanting power,
Was taken and imprisoned in the Tower.
But by a sleepy drink which she prepared,
And at a banquet given to his guard,
He makes escape: to whom to France she sends;
Who thence to her his service recommends.

THOUGH such sweet comfort comes not now from her,
As England's Queen hath sent to Mortimer;
Yet what that wants (may it my power approve,
If lines can bring) this shall supply with love.
Methinks affliction should not fright me so,
Nor should resume those sundry shapes of woe;
But when I fain would find the cause of this,
Thy absence shows me where my error is.

Oft when I think of thy departing hence,
Sad sorrow then possesseth every sense :
But finding thy dear blood preserved thereby,
And in thy life my long-wished liberty,
With that sweet thought myself I only please
Amidst my grief, which sometimes gives me ease :
Thus do extremest ills a joy possess,
And one woe makes another woe seem less.

    That blessèd night, that mild-aspected hour,
Wherein thou madst escape out of the Tower,
Shall consecrated evermore remain ;
Some gentle planet in that hour did reign,
And shall be happy in the birth of men,
Which was chief Lord of the Ascendant then.
[a] O how I feared that sleepy juice I sent
Might yet want power to further thine intent!
Or that some unseen mystery might lurk,
Which wanting order kindly should not work :
Oft did I wish those dreadful poisoned lees
Which closed the ever-waking dragon's eyes ;
Or I had had those sense-bereaving stalks
That grow in shady Proserpine's dark walks ;
Or those black weeds on Lethe banks below,
Or lunary that doth on Latmos flow.
Oft did I fear this moist and foggy clime,
Or that the earth, waxed barren now with time,
Should not have herbs to help me in this case,
Such as do thrive on India's parchèd face.

    That morrow, when the blessèd sun did rise
And shut the lids of all Heaven's lesser eyes,
Forth from my palace by a secret stair
[b] I stole to Thames, as though to take the air;
And asked the gentle flood as it doth glide
If thou didst pass or perish by the tide ?

If thou didst perish, I desire the stream
To lay thee softly on his silver team,
And bring thee to me to the quiet shore,
That with his tears thou mightst have some tears more.
When suddenly doth rise a rougher gale,
With that methinks the troubled waves look pale,
And sighing with that little gust that blows,
With this remembrance seem to knit their brows.
Even as this sudden passion doth affright me,
The cheerful sun breaks from a cloud to light me;
Then doth the bottom evident appear,
As it would show me that thou wast not there:
Whenas the water flowing where I stand,
Doth seem to tell me thou art safe on land.
  c Did Boulogne once a festival prepare,
For England, Almain, Sicil, and Navarre?
When France envíed those buildings only blest,
Graced with the orgies of my bridal feast,
That English Edward should refuse my bed,
For that lascivious shameless Ganymed;
d And in my place upon his regal throne
To set that girl-boy, wanton Gaveston?
Betwixt the feature of my face and his
My glass assures me no such difference is,
e That a foul witch's bastard should thereby
Be thought more worthy of his love than I.
What doth avail us to be Princes' heirs,
When we can boast our birth is only theirs?
When base dissembling flatterers shall deceive us
Of all that our great ancestors did leave us,
f And of our princely jewels and our dowers
Let us enjoy the least of what is ours;   [crowns,
Where minions' heads must wear our monarchs'
To raise up dunghills with our famous towns:

Those beggar-brats wrapt in our rich perfumes,
Their buzzard-wings imped with our eagles' plumes,
g And matched with the brave issue of our blood,
Ally the kingdom to their craven brood.
Did Longshanks purchase with his conquering hand
  h Albania, Gascoine, Cambria, Ireland,
That young Carnarvon, his unhappy son,
i Should give away all that his father won,
To back a stranger, proudly bearing down
The brave allies and branches of the Crown?
j And did great Edward on his deathbed give
This charge to them which afterwards should live,
That that proud Gascoine, banishéd the land,
No more should tread upon the English sand?
And have these great lords in the quarrel stood,
And sealed his last will with their dearest blood,
k That after all this fearful massacre,
The fall of Beauchamp, Lacy, Lancaster,
Another faithless favourite should arise
To cloud the sun of our nobilities?
l And gloried I in Gaveston's great fall
That now a Spenser should succeed in all?
And that his ashes should another breed,
Which in his place and empire should succeed;
That wanting one a kingdom's wealth to spend,
Of what that left this now shall make an end;
To waste all that our father won before,
Nor leave our son a sword to conquer more?
Thus but in vain we fondly do resist
Where power can do even all things as it list,
And of our right with tyrants to debate
Lendeth them means to weaken our estate;
Whilst Parliaments must remedy their wrongs,
And we must wait for what to us belongs;

Our wealth but fuel to their fond excess,
And all our fasts must feast their wantonness.
   Thinkest thou our wrongs then insufficient are
To move our brother to religious war ?
ᵐ And if they were, yet Edward doth detain
Homage for Pontieu, Guyne, and Aquitaine :
And if not that, yet hath he broke the truce ;
Thus all occur to put back all excuse.
The sister's wrong, joined with the brother's right,
Methinks might urge him in this cause to fight.
Be all those people senseless of our harms,
Who for our country oft have managed arms ?
Is the brave Norman's courage quite forgot ?
Have the bold Britons lost the use of shot ?
The big-boned Almans and stout Brabanders,
Their warlike pikes and sharp-edged scimitars ?
Or do the Pickards let their crossbows lie,
Once like the Centaurs of old Thessaly ?
Or if a valiant leader be their lack,
Where thou art present who should beat them back ?
   I do conjure thee by what is most dear,
By that great name of famous Mortimer,
ⁿ By ancient Wigmore's honourable crest,
The tombs where all thy famous grandsires rest,
Or if than these what more may thee approve,
Even by those vows of thy unfeigned love ;
In all thou canst to stir the Christian King,
By foreign arms some comfort yet to bring
To curb the power of traitors that rebel
Against the right of princely Isabel.
Vain, witless woman, why should I desire
To add more heat to thy immortal fire ?
To urge thee by the violence of hate
To shake the pillars of thine own estate

When whatsoever we intend to do,
Our most misfortune ever sorteth to;
And nothing else remains for us beside
But tears and coffins only to provide?
°When stil'. so long as Burrough bears that name,
Time shall not blot out our deservéd shame;
And whilst clear Trent her wonted course shall keep,
For our sad fall she evermore shall weep.
All see our ruin on our backs is thrown,
And we too weak to bear it out are grown.
ᴾ Torlton, that should our business direct,
The general foe doth vehemently suspect:
For dangerous things get hardly to their end,
Whereon so many watchfully attend.
Why should I say? My griefs do still renew,
And but begin when I should bid adieu.
Few be my words, but manifold my woe,
And still I stay the more I strive to go.
Then till fair time some greater good affords,
Take my love's payment in these airy words.

ANNOTATIONS OF THE CHRONICLE HISTORY.

ᵃ "O, how I feared that sleepy juice I sent,
      Might yet want power to further mine intent!'

Mortimer being in the Tower, and ordaining a feast in honour of his birthday, as he pretended, and inviting thereunto Sir Stephen Segrave, Constable of the Tower, with the rest of the officers belonging to the same, he gave them a sleepy drink, provided him by the Queen, by which means he got liberty for his escape.

ᵇ "I stole to Thames, as though to take the air,
      And asked the gentle flood as it doth glide."

Mortimer being got out of the Tower, swam the river of Thames into Kent, whereof she having intelligence, doubteth of his strength to escape, by reason of his long imprisonment, being almost the space of three years.

HEROICAL EPISTLES. 171

^c "Did Boulogne once a festival prepare
For England, Almain, Sicil, and Navarre?"

Edward Carnarvon, the first Prince of Wales of the English blood, married Isabel daughter of Philip the Fair at Boulogne, in the presence of the Kings of Almain, Navarre, and Sicil, with the chief nobility of France and England : which marriage was solemnized with exceeding pomp and magnificence.

^d "And in my place, upon his legal throne,
To let that girl-boy, wanton Gaveston."

Noting the effeminacy and luxurious wantonness of Gaveston, the King's minion, his behaviour and attire ever so woman-like, to please the eye of his lascivious master.

^e "That a foul witch's bastard should thereby."

It was urged by the Queen and the nobility, in the disgrace of Pierce Gaveston, that his mother was convicted of witchcraft, and burned for the same, and that Pierce had bewitched the King.

^f "And of our princely jewels and our dowers,
Let us enjoy the least of what is ours."

A complaint of the prodigality of King Edward, giving unto Gaveston the jewels and treasure which was left him by the ancient Kings of England, and enriching him with the goodly manor of Wallingford, assigned as parcel of the dower to the Queens of this famous isle.

^g "And matched with the brave issue of our blood,
Ally the kingdom to their craven brood."

Edward the Second gave to Pierce Gaveston in marriage the daughter of Gilbert Clare, Earl of Gloucester, begot of the King's sister Joan of Acres, married to the said Earl of Gloucester.

^h "Albania, Gascoine, Cambria, Ireland."

Albania, Scotland, so called of Albanact, the second son of Brutus, and Cambria, Wales, so called of Camber, the third son. The four realms and countries brought in subjection by Edward Longshanks.

ⁱ "Should give away all that his father won,
To back a stranger, &c."

King Edward offered his right in France to Charles, his brother-in-law, and his right in Scotland to Robert Bruce, to be aided against the Barons in the quarrel of Pierce Gaveston.

j "And did great Edward on his deathbed give."

Edward Longshanks, on his deathbed at Carlisle, commanded young Edward his son, on his blessing, not to call back Gaveston, which, for the misguiding of the Prince's youth, was before banished by the whole council of the land.

k "That after all this fearful massacre,
The fall of Beauchamp, Lacy, Lancaster."

Thomas Earl of Lancaster, Guy Earl of Warwick, and Henry Earl of Lincoln, who had taken their oaths before the deceased King at his death to withstand his son Edward, if he should call Gaveston from exile, being a thing which he much feared; now seeing Edward to violate his father's commandment, rise in arms against the King, which was the cause of the civil war, and the ruin of so many Princes.

l "And gloried I in Gaveston's great fall,
That now a Spenser should succeed in all?"

The two Hugh Spensers, the father and the son, after the death of Gaveston, became the great favourites of the King, the son being created by him Lord Chamberlain, and the father Earl of Winchester.

m "And if they were, yet Edward doth detain .
Homage for Pontieu, Guine, and Aquitaine."

Edward Longshanks did homage for those cities and territories to the French king, which Edward the Second neglecting, moved the French king, by the subornation of Mortimer, to seize those countries into his hands.

n "By ancient Wigmore's honourable crest."

Wigmore, in the Marches of Wales, was the ancient house of the Mortimers, that noble and courageous family.

o "When still so long as Burrough bears that name."

The Queen remembereth the great overthrow given to the Barons by Andrew Herckley, Earl of Carlisle, at Burrough Bridge, after the battle at Burton.

p "Torlton, that should our business direct."

This was Adam Torlton, Bishop of Hereford, that great politician, who so highly favoured the faction of the Queen and Mortimer, whose evil counsel afterward wrought the destruction of the King.

MORTIMER TO QUEEN ISABEL.

As thy salutes my sorrows do adjourn,
So back to thee their interest I return,
Though not in so great bounty, I confess,
As thy heroic princely lines express:
For how should comfort issue from the breath
ᵃ Of one condemned and long lodged up for death?
From murder's rage thou didst me once reprieve,
Now in exile my hopes thou dost revive:
ᵇ Twice all was taken, twice they all didst give,
And thus twice dead, thou makest me twice to live:
This double life of mine, your only due,
You gave to me, I give it back to you.
   Ne'er my escape had I adventured thus,
As did the shy attempting Dedalus;
And yet to give more safety to my flight,
Did make a night of day, a day of night:
Nor had I backed the proud aspiring wall,
Which held without my hopes, within my fall,
ᶜ Leaving the cords to tell 'where I had gone,
For gazers with much fear to look upon;
But that thy beauty, by a power divine,
Breathed a new life into this spirit of mine,
Drawn by the sun of thy celestial eyes,
With fiery wings, which bare me through the skies.
The heavens did seem the charge of me to take,
And sea and land befriend me for thy sake;
Thames stopped his tide to make me way to go,
As thou hadst charged him that it should be so:
The hollow murmuring winds their due time kept,
As they had rocked the world while all things slept;

One billow bare me, and another drave me,
This strove to help me, and that strove to save me:
The bristling reeds moved with soft gales did chide me,
As they would tell me that they meant to hide me:
The pale-faced night beheld thy heavy cheer,
And would not let one little star appear,
But over all her smoky mantle hurled
And in thick vapours muffled up the world:
And the sad air became so calm and still
As it had been obedient to my will;
And everything disposed it to my rest,
As on the seas when the halcyon builds her nest.
When those rough waves, which late with fury rushed,
Slide smoothly on and suddenly are hushed:
Nor Neptune lets his surges out so long
As Nature is in bringing forth her young.

   [d] Ne'er let the Spensers glory in my chance,
In that I live an exile here in France,
That I from England banishéd should be,
But England rather banishéd from me: [bear,
More were her wont, France our great blood should
Than England's loss can be to Mortimer.

   [e] My grandsire was the first since Arthur's reign
That the Round Table rectified again:
To whose great Court at Kenilworth did come
The peerless knighthood of all Christendom,
Whose princely order honoured England more
Than all the conquests she achieved before.

   Never durst Scot set foot on English ground,
Nor on his back did English bear a wound,
Whilst Wigmore flourished in our princely hopes,
And whilst our ensigns marched with Edward's troops:
[f] Whilst famous Longshanks' bones, in Fortune's scorn,
As sacred relics to the field were borne:

Nor ever did the valiant English doubt
Whilst our brave battles guarded them about;
Nor did our wives and woful mothers mourn
ᵍ The English blood that stainéd Bannockburn,
Whilst with his minions sporting in his tent
Whole days and nights in banqueting were spent,
Until the Scots, which under safeguard stood,
Made lavish havoc of the English blood,
Whose battered helms lay scattered on the shore,
Where they in conquest had been borne before.
 A thousand kingdoms will we seek from far,
As many nations waste with civil war,
Where the dishevelled ghastly sea-nymph sings,
Or well-rigged ships shall stretch their swelling wings,
And drag their anchors through the sandy foam,
About the world in every clime to roam,
And those unchristened countries call our own,
Where scarce the name of England hath been known:
ʰ And in the Dead Sea sink our house's fame,
From whose vast depth we first derived our name,
Before foul black-mouthed infamy shall sing
That Mortimer ere stooped unto a King.
And we will turn stern-visaged Fury back,
To seek his spoil who sought our utter sack,
And come to beard him in our native isle,
Ere he march forth to follow our exile:
And after all these boisterous stormy shocks,
Yet will we grapple with the chalky rocks;
Nor will we steal, like pirates or like thieves,
From mountains, forests, or sea-bordering cleeves,
But fright the air with terror, when we come,
Of the stern trumpet and the bellowing drum,
And in the field advance our plumy crest,
And march upon fair England's flowery breast.

And Thames, which once we for our life did swim,
Shaking our dewy tresses on his brim,
Shall bear my navy vaunting in her pride,
Falling from Thanet with the powerful tide;
Which fertile Essex and fair Kent shall see,
Spreading her flags along the pleasant Lee,
When on her stemming poop she proudly bears
The famous ensigns of the Belgic Peers.
[i] And for that hateful sacrilegious sin
Which by the Pope he stands accursèd in,
The Canon text shall have a common gloss,
Receipts in parcels shall be paid in gross :   [take,
This doctrine preached, "Who from the Church doth
At least shall treble restitution make."
For which Rome sends her curses out from far,
Through the stern throat of terror-breathing war ;
Till to the unpeopled shores she brings supplies
[j] Of those industrious Roman colonies,
And for his homage, by the which of old
Proud Edward Guyne and Aquitaine doth hold,
[k] Charles by invasive arms again shall take,
And send the English forces o'er the lake.
When Edward's fortune stands upon this chance,
To lose in England or to forfeit France ;
And all those towns great Longshanks left his son,
Now lost, which once he fortunately won,
Within their strong portcullised ports shall lie,
And from their walls his sieges shall defy :
And by that firm and undissolvèd knot,   [Scot,
Betwixt their neighbouring French and bordering
Bruce shall bring on his Redshanks from the seas,
From the islèd Orcads and the Eubides,
And to his western havens give free pass,
To land the kerne and Irish galiglass,

Marching from Tweed to swelling Humber sands,
Wafting along the Northern netherlands.
And wanting those which should his power sustain,
Consumed with slaughter in his bloody reign,
Our warlike sword shall drive him from his throne,
Where he shall lie for us to tread upon.
  And those great lords, now after their attaints,
Canonizéd amongst the English saints,
And by the superstitious people thought
That by their relics miracles are wrought ;
And think that flood much virtue doth retain
Which took the blood of famous Bohun slain ;
Continuing the remembrance of the thing,
Shall make the people more abhor their King.
  Nor shall a Spenser, be he ne'er so great,
Possess our Wigmore, our renownéd seat,
To raze the ancient trophies of our race,
With our deserts their monuments to grace ;
Nor shall he lead our valiant marchers forth,
To make the Spensers famous in the North ;
Nor be the guardians of the British pales,
Defending England and preserving Wales.
  At first our troubles easily reculed,
But now grown headstrong, hardly to be ruled ;
Deliberate counsel needs us to direct,
Where not even plainness frees us from suspect :
By those mishaps our errors that attend,
Let us our faults ingenuously amend,
Then, dear, repress all peremptory spleen,
Be more than woman, as you are a Queen :
Smother those sparks which quickly else would burn,
Till time produce what now it doth adjourn.
Till when, great Queen, I leave you, though a while,
Live you in rest, nor pity my exile.

ANNOTATIONS OF THE CHRONICLE HISTORY.

a "Of one condemned and long lodged up for death."

Roger Mortimer, Lord of Wigmore, had stood publicly condemned for his insurrection with Thomas, Earl of Lancaster, and Bohun, Earl of Hertford, by the space of three months' stand, as the report went, the day of his execution was determined to have been shortly, which he prevented by his escape.

b "Twice all was taken, twice thou all didst give."

At what time the two Mortimers, this Roger, Lord of Wigmore, and his uncle, Roger Mortimer the elder, were apprehended in the West, the Queen, by means of Torlton, Bishop of Hereford, and Becke, Bishop of Durham and Patriarch of Jerusalem, being then both mighty in the State, upon the submission of the Mortimers, somewhat pacified the King; and now, secondly, she wrought means for his escape.

c "Leaving the cords to tell where I had gone."

With strong ladders made of cords, provided him for the purpose, he escaped out of the Tower; which when the same were found fastened to the walls, in such a desperate attempt, they bred astonishment in the beholders.

d "Ne'er let the Spensers glory in my chance."

The two Hugh Spensers, the father and the son, then being so highly favoured of the King, knew that their greatest safety came by his exile, whose high and turbulent spirit could never brook any co-rival in greatness.

e "My grandsire was the first since Arthur's reign
That the Round Table rectified again."

Roger Mortimer, called the great Lord Mortimer, grandfather to this Roger, which was afterward the first Earl of March, erected again the Round Table at Kenilworth, after the ancient order of King Arthur's Table, with the retinue of a hundred knights, and a hundred ladies in his house, for the entertaining of such adventurers as came thither from all parts of Christendom.

f "Whilst famous Longshanks' bones, in Fortune's scorn."

Edward Longshanks willed at his death that his body should be boiled the flesh from the bones, and that the bones should be borne to the wars in Scotland, which he was persuaded unto by a prophecy, which told that the English should still be fortunate in conquest so long as his bones were carried in the field.

g "The English blood that stained Bannockburn."

In the great voyage Edward the Second made against the Scots, at the battle of Striveling, near unto the river of Bannockburn in Scotland, there was in the English camp such banqueting and excess, such riot and misorder, that the Scots (who in the meantime laboured for advantage) gave to the English a great overthrow.

h "And in the Dead Sea sink our house's fame,
From whose, &c."

Mortimer, so called of *Mare mortuum*, and in French Mortimer, in English the Dead Sea, which is said to be where Sodom and Gomorrah once were, before they were destroyed with fire from heaven.

i "And for that hateful sacrilegious sin,
Which by the Pope he stands accursèd in."

Gaustellimus and Lucas, two Cardinals, sent into England from Pope Clement, to appease the ancient hate between the King and Thomas, Earl of Lancaster; to whose embassy the King seemed to yield, but after their departure he went back from his promises, for the which he was accursed at Rome.

j "Of those industrious Roman colonies."

A colony is a sort or number of people that come to inhabit a place before not inhabited; whereby he seems here to prophesy of the subversion of the land, the Pope joining with the power of other princes against Edward for the breach of his promise.

k " Charles by invasive arms again shall take."

Charles, the French king, moved by the wrong done unto his sister, seizeth the Provinces which belonged to the King of England into his hands, stirred the rather thereto by Mortimer, who solicited her cause in France.

l " And those great lords, now after their attaints,
Canonized among the English saints."

After the death of Thomas, Earl of Lancaster, at Pomfret, the people imagined great miracles to be done by his relics, as they did of the body of Bohun, Earl of Hertford, slain at Burrough Bridge.

QUEEN ISABEL

TO

RICHARD THE SECOND.

THE ARGUMENT.

Richard the Second wrongfully deposed
By Henry, Duke of Hertford, and enclosed
In Pomfret Castle ; Isabel, the Queen,
To the neglected King, who having seen
His disinvesting and disastrous chance,
To Charles, her father, shipped again for France,
Where for her husband grieved and discontent,
Thence this Epistle to King Richard sent,
By which when he her sorrow doth descry
He to the same as sadly doth reply.

As doth the yearly augur of the spring,
In depth of woe thus I my sorrow sing ;
My tunes with sighs yet ever mixed among,
A doleful burthen to a heavy song ;
Words issue forth to find my grief some way,
Tears overtake them and do bid them stay ;
Thus whilst one strives to keep the other back,
Both once too forward, soon are both too slack.
 If fatal Pomfret hath in former time
Nourished the grief of that unnatural clime,
Thither I send my sorrows to be fed ;
Than where first born where fitter to be bred ?
They unto France be aliens and unknown,
England from her doth challenge these her own.
They say all mischief cometh from the North ;
It is too true, my fall doth set it forth :

But why should I thus limit grief a place,
When all the world is filled with our disgrace?
And we in bonds thus striving to contain it,
The more resists the more we do restrain it.
   [a] Oh, how even yet I hate those wretched eyes,
And in my glass oft call them faithless spies!
Prepared for Richard, that unawares did look
Upon that traitor Henry Bolingbrooke:
But that excess of joy my sense bereaved
So much my sight had never been deceived.
Oh, how unlike to my loved lord was he,
Whom rashly I, sweet Richard, took for thee!
I might have seen the courser's self did lack
That princely rider to bestride his back;
He that since Nature her great work began,
She only made the mirror of a man,
That when she meant to form some matchless limb,
Still for a pattern took some part of him,
And jealous of her cunning, brake the mould,
When she in him had done the best she could.
   Oh, let that day be guilty of all sin
That is to come or heretofore hath been,
[b] Wherein great Norfolk's forward course was stayed,
To prove the treasons he to Hertford laid.
When with stern fury both these Dukes enraged,
Their warlike gloves at Coventry engaged,
When first thou didst repeal thy former grant,
Sealed to brave Mowbray as thy combatant:
From his unnumbered hours let time divide it,
Lest in his minutes he should hap to hide it;
Yet on his brow continually to bear it,
That when it comes all other hours may fear it,
And all ill-boding planets, by consent,
In it may hold their dreadful Parliament:

Be it in Heaven's decrees enrolléd thus,
Black, dismal, fatal, inauspicious.
Proud Hertford then in height of all his pride,
Under great Mowbray's valiant hand had died,
And never had frcm banishment retired ;
The fatal brand wherewith our Troy was fired.
^c Oh ! why did Charles relieve his needy state ?
A vagabond and straggling runagate ;
And in his Court with grace did entertain
That vagrant exile, that vile bloody Cain,
Who with a thousand mothers' curses went,
Marked with the brand of ten years' banishment.

^d When thou to Ireland tookest thy last farewell,
Millions of knees upon the pavements fell,
And everywhere the applauding echoes ring
The joyful shouts that did salute a King.
Thy parting hence the pomp that did adorn,
Was vanquished quite whenas thou didst return :
Who to my lord one look vouchsafed to lend ?
Then all too few on Hertford to attend.
Princes, like suns, be evermore in sight,
All see the clouds betwixt them and their light :
Yet they which lighten all down from their skies,
See not the clouds offending others' eyes,
And deem their noontide is desired of all,
When all expect clear changes by their fall.

What colour seems to shadow Hertford's claim,
When law and right his father's hopes do maim ?
^e Affirmed by Churchmen, who should bear no hate,
That John of Gaunt was illegitimate ;
Whom his reputed mother's tongue did spot,
By a base Flemish boor to be begot ;
Whom Edward's eaglets mortally did shun,
Daring with them to gaze against the sun :

Where lawful right and conquest doth allow
A triple crown on Richard's princely brow ;
Three kingly lions bear his bloody field,
ᶠ No bastard's mark doth blot his conquering shield :
Never durst he attempt our hapless shore,
Nor set his foot on fatal Ravenspore ;
Nor durst his slugging hulks approach the strand,
Nor stoop a top as signal to the land,
Had not the Percies promised aid to bring
Against their oath unto their lawful King,
ᵍ Against their faith unto our Crown's true heir,
Their valiant kinsman, Edmund Mortimer.
   When I to England came, a world of eyes
Like stars attended on my fair arise,
Which now, alas, like angry planets frown,
And are all set before my going down :
The smooth-faced air did on my coming smile,
But I with storms am driven to exile :
But Bolingbrooke devised we thus should part,
Fearing two sorrows should possess one heart,
To add to our affliction, to deny
That one poor comfort left our misery,
He had before divorced thy Crown and thee,
Which might suffice and not to widow me ;
But so to prove the utmost of his hate,
To part us in this miserable state.
ʰ Oh, would Aumerle had sunk when he betrayed
The plot which once that noble Abbot laid,
When he infringed the oath which he first took,
For thy revenge on perjured Bolingbrooke ;
And been the ransom of our friends' dear blood,
Untimely lost and for the earth too good :
And we untimely do bewail their state,
They gone too soon, and we remain too late.

And though with tears I from my lord depart,
This curse on Hertford fall, to ease my heart:
If the foul breach of a chaste nuptial bed
May bring a curse, my curse light on his head:
If murder's guilt with blood may deeply stain,
[i] Greene, Scroope, and Bushy dye his fault ingrain:
If perjury may Heaven's pure gates debar,
[j] Damned be the oath he made at Doncaster:
If the deposing of a lawful King,
Thy curse condemn him, if no other thing:
If these disjoined for vengeance cannot call,
Let them united strongly curse him all.
And for the Percies, Heaven may hear my prayer,
That Bolingbrooke, now placed in Richard's chair,
Such cause of woe to their proud wives may be
As those rebellious lords have been to me.
And that coy dame, who now controlleth all,
And in her pomp triumpheth in my fall,
For her great lord may water her sad eyne
With as salt tears as I have done for mine.
[k] And mourn for Henry Hotspur, her dear son,
As I for my dear Mortimer have done;
And as I am, so succourless be sent
Lastly to taste perpetual banishment.
Then lose thy care, when first thy Crown was lost,
Sell it so dearly, for it dearly cost:
And since it did of liberty deprive thee,
Burying thy hope, let nothing else outlive thee.
But hard, God knows, with sorrow doth it go,
When woe becomes a comforter to woe:
Yet much methinks of comfort I could say,
If from my heart some fears were rid away;
Something there is that danger still doth show,
But what it is, that Heaven alone doth know:

Grief to itself most dreadful doth appear,
And never yet was sorrow void of fear ;
But yet in death doth sorrow hope the best
And, Richard, thus I wish thee happy rest.

ANNOTATIONS OF THE CHRONICLE HISTORY.

a "If fatal Pomfret hath in former time."

Pomfret Castle, ever a fatal place to the Princes of England, and most ominous to the blood of Plantagenet.

b "Oh, how even yet I hate these wretched eyes,
And in my glass, &c."

When Bolingbrooke returned to London from the West, bringing Richard a prisoner with him, the Queen, who little knew of her husband's hard success, stayed to behold his coming in, little thinking to have seen her husband thus led in triumph by his foe ; and now seemed to hate her eyes, that so much had graced her mortal enemy.

c "Wherein great Norfolk's forward course was stayed."

She remembereth the meeting of the two Dukes of Hertford and Norfolk at Coventry, urging the justness of Mowbray's quarrel against the Duke of Hertford, and the faithful assurance of his victory.

d "Oh ! why did Charles relieve his needy state?
A vagabond, &c."

Charles, the French king, her father, received the Duke of Hertford into his Court, and relieved him in France, being so nearly allied as cousin. german to King Richard, his son-in-law ; which he did simply, little thinking that he should after return into England, and dispossess King Richard of the crown.

e "When thou to Ireland tookst thy last farewell."

King Richard made a voyage with his army into Ireland against Onell and Mackmur, which rebelled ; at what time Henry entered here at home and robbed him of all kingly dignity.

f "Affirmed by Churchmen, who should bear no hate,
That John of Gaunt was illegitimate."

William Wickham, in the great quarrel betwixt John of Gaunt and the clergy, of mere spite and malice, as it should seem, reported that the

Queen confessed to him on her deathbed, being then her confessor, that John of Gaunt was the son of a Fleming, and that she was brought to bed of a woman-child at Gaunt, which was smothered in the cradle by mischance, and that she obtained this child of a poor woman, making the King believe it was her own, greatly fearing his displeasure. Fox ex Chron. Alban.

^g " No bastard's mark doth blot his conquering shield."

Showing the true and indubitate birth of Richard, his right unto the Crown of England, as carrying the arms without blot or difference.

^h " Against their faith unto the Crown's true heir,
Their valiant kinsman, &c."

Edmund Mortimer, Earl of March, son of Earl Roger Mortimer, who was son to Lady Philip, daughter to Lionel, Duke of Clarence, the third son to King Edward the Third, which Edmund (King Richard going into Ireland) was proclaimed heir-apparent to the Crown; whose aunt, called Ellinor, this Lord Percy had married.

ⁱ "O would Aumerle had sunk, when he betrayed
The plot which once the noble Abbot laid."

The Abbot of Westminster had plotted the death of King Henry to have been done at a tilt at Oxford. Of which confederacy there was John Holland, Duke of Exeter, Thomas Holland, Duke of Surrey, the Duke of Aumerle, Montacute, Earl of Salisbury, Spenser, Earl of Gloucester, the Bishop of Carlisle, Sir Thomas Blunt; these all had bound themselves one to another by indenture to perform it, but were all betrayed by the Duke of Aumerle.

^j " Scroope, Green, and Bushy, dye his fault ingrain."

Henry, going towards the Castle of Flint, where King Richard was, caused Scroope, Green, and Bushy to be executed at Bristol, as vile persons, who had seduced the King to this lascivious and wicked life.

^k " Damned be the oath he made at Doncaster."

After Henry's exile, at his return into England, he took his oath at Doncaster upon the sacrament, not to claim the Crown or kingdom of England, but only the Dukedom of Lancaster, his own proper right and the right of his wife.

^l "And mourn for Henry Hotspur, her dear son,
As I for my, &c."

This was the brave courageous Henry Hotspur, that obtained so many victories against the Scots; who after falling out right with the curse of Queen Isabel, was slain by Henry at the battle at Shrewsbury.

RICHARD THE SECOND

TO

QUEEN ISABEL.

WHAT can my Queen but hope for from this hand
That it should write, which never could command,
A kingdom's greatness think how he should sway,
That wholesome counsel never could obey :
Ill this rude hand did guide a sceptre then,
Worse now, I fear me, it will rule a pen.
  How shall I call myself, or by what name,
To make thee know from whence these letters came ?
Not from thy husband, for my hateful life
Makes thee a widow, being yet a wife :
Nor from a King, that title I have lost,
Now of that name proud Bolingbrooke may boast :
What I have been doth but this comfort bring,
No words so woful as " I was a King."
This lawless life, which first procured my hate,
ª This tongue, which then renounced my regal state,
This abject soul of mine consenting to it,
This hand that was the instrument to do it ;
All these be witness that I now deny
All princely types, all kingly sovereignty.
  Didst thou for my sake leave thy father's Court,
Thy famous country and thy princely port,
And undertookst to travel dangerous ways,
Driven by awkward winds and boist'rous seas ?
ᵇ And leftst great Bourbon for thy love to me,
Who sued in marriage to be linked to thee,

Offering for dower the countries neighbouring nigh,
Of fruitful Almain and rich Burgundy?
Didst thou all this that England should receive thee,
To miserable banishment to leave thee?
And in my downfall and my fortune's wrack
Thus to thy country to convey thee back?
    When quiet sleep, the heavy heart's relief,
Hath rested sorrow, somewhat lessened grief,
My passéd greatness into mind I call,
And think this while I dreaméd of my fall:
With this conceit my sorrows I beguile,
That my fair Queen is but withdrawn a while,
And my attendants in some chamber by,
As in the height of my prosperity,
Calling aloud and asking who is there?
The echo answering, tells me woe is there;
And when mine arms would gladly thee enfold,
I clip the pillow and the place is cold:
Which when my waking eyes precisely view,
'Tis a true token that it is too true.
    As many minutes as in the hours there be,
So many hours each minute seems to me;
Each hour a day, morn, noontide, and a set
Each day a year, with miseries complete;
A winter, spring-time, summer, and a fall.
All seasons varying, but unseasoned all:
In endless woe my thread of life thus wears,
In minutes, hours, days, months, to lingering years.
    They praise the summer that enjoy the South,
Pomfret is closéd in the North's cold mouth;
There pleasant summer dwelleth all the year,
Frost-starvéd winter doth inhabit here:
·A place wherein despair may fitly dwell,
Sorrow best suiting with a cloudy cell.

c When Hertford had his judgment of exile,
Saw I the people's murmuring the while ;
The uncertain commons touched with inward care,
As though his sorrows mutually they bare :
Fond women and scarce-speaking children mourn,
Bewail his parting, wishing his return.
d That I was forced to abridge his banished years
When they bedewed his footsteps with their tears ;
Yet by example could not learn to know
To what his greatness by their love might grow,
e But Henry boasts of our achievements done,
Bearing the trophies our great fathers won,
And all the story of our famous war
Must grace the annals of great Lancaster.
  f Seven goodly scions in their spring did flourish,
Which one self-root brought forth, one stock did
    nourish.
g Edward the top-branch of that golden tree,
Nature in him her utmost power did see,
Who from the bud still blossoméd so fair,
As all might judge what fruit it meant to bear :
But I his graft, of every weed o'ergrown,
And from our kind as refuse forth am thrown.
h We from our grandsire stood in one degree,
But after Edward, John the young'st of three,
Might princely Wales beget a son so base,
That to Gaunt's issue should give sovereign place ?
i He that from France brought John his prisoner
    home,
As those great Cæsars did their spoils to Rome,
j Whose name obtained by his fatal hand
Was ever fearful to that conquered land :
His fame increasing, purchased in those wars,
Can scarcely now be bounded with the stars ;

With him is valour from the base world fled,
Or here in me it is extinguishéd,
Who for his virtue, and his conquests' sake
Posterity a demigod shall make ;
And judge this vile and abject spirit of mine
Could not proceed from temper so divine.
   What earthly humour or what vulgar eye
Can look so low as on our misery ?
When Bolingbrooke is mounted to our throne,
And makes that his which we but called our own ;
Into our councils he himself intrudes,
And who but Henry with the multitudes ?
His power degrades, his dreadful frown disgraceth,
He throws them down whom our advancement placeth ;
As my disabled and unworthy hand
Never had power belonging to command.
He treads our sacred tables in the dust,
^k And proves our Acts of Parliament unjust ;
As though he hated that it should be said
That such a law by Richard once was made :
Whilst I, deprest before his greatness, lie
Under the weight of hate and infamy.
My back a footstool Bolingbrooke to raise,
My looseness mocked and hateful by his praise,
Outlive mine honour, bury my estate,
And leave myself nought but my people's hate.
   Sweet Queen, I'll take all counsel thou canst give,
So that thou bidst me neither hope nor live :
Succour that comes when ill hath done his worst,
But sharpens grief to make us more accurst.
Comfort is now unpleasing to mine ear,
Past cure, past care, my bed become my bier :
Since now misfortune humbleth us so long,
Till Heaven be grown unmindful of our wrong ;

Yet it forbid my wrongs should ever die,
But still remembered to posterity:
And let the Crown be fatal that he wears,
And ever wet with woful mothers' tears.
Thy curse on Percy, angry Heavens prevent,
Who have not one curse left on him unspent,
To scourge the world, now borrowing of my store,
As rich of woe as I a King am poor.
Then cease, dear Queen, my sorrows to bewail,
My wound's too great for pity now to heal;
Age stealeth on whilst thou complainest thus,
My griefs be mortal and infectious:
Yet better fortunes thy fair youth may try
That follow thee. which still from me doth fly.

ANNOTATIONS OF THE CHRONICLE HISTORY.

a " This tongue, which then renounced my regal state."

Richard the Second, at the resignation of the Crown to the Duke of Hertford in the Tower of London, delivering the same with his own hand, there confessed his disability to govern, utterly renouncing all kingly authority.

b " And left great Bourbon for thy love to me."

Before the Princess Isabel was married to the King, Lewis, Duke of Bourbon, sued to have had her in marriage; which was thought he had obtained, if this motion had not fallen out in the meantime. This Duke of Bourbon sued again to have received her at her coming into France, after the imprisonment of King Richard, but King Charles, her father, then crossed him, as before, and gave her to Charles, son to the Duke of Orleans.

c " When Hertford had his judgment of exile."

When the combat should have been at Coventry betwixt Henry, Duke of Hertford, and Thomas, Duke of Norfolk (where Hertford was adjudged to banishment for ten years), the commons exceedingly lamented, so greatly was he ever favoured of the people.

^d "Then being forced to abridge his banished years."

When the Duke came to take his leave of the King, being then at Eltham, the King, to please the commons rather than for any love he bare to Hertford, repealed four years of his banishment.

^e "But Henry boasts of our achievements done."

Henry, the eldest son of John, Duke of Lancaster, at the first, Earl of Derby, then created Duke of Hertford; after the death of the Duke John, his father was Duke of Lancaster and Hertford, Earl of Derby, Leicester, and Lincoln; and after he had obtained the Crown, was called by the name of Bolingbrooke, which is a town in Lincolnshire; as usually all the Kings of England bare the name of the place where they were born.

^f "Seven goodly scions in their spring did flourish."

Edward the Third had seven sons, Edward Prince of Wales, after called the Black Prince; William of Hatfield, the second; Lionel, Duke of Clarence, the third; John of Gaunt, Duke of Lancaster, the fourth; Edmund of Langley, Duke of York, the fifth; Thomas of Woodstock, Duke of Gloucester, the sixth; William of Windsor, the seventh.

^g "Edward the top-branch of that golden tree."

Truly boasting himself to be the eldest son of Edward the Black Prince.

^h "Yet after Edward, John the youngest of three."

As disabling Henry Bolingbrooke, being but the son of the fourth brother, William and Lionel being both before John of Gaunt.

ⁱ "He that from France brought John his prisoner home."

Edward the Black Prince taking John, King of France, prisoner at the battle of Poictiers, brought him into England, where at the Savoy he died.

^j "Whose name achieved by his fatal hand."

Called the Black Prince, not so much of his complexion, as of the famous battles he fought.

^k "And proves our Acts of Parliament unjust."

In the next Parliament, after Richard's resignation of the Crown, Henry caused to be annihilated all the laws made in the Parliament, called the wicked Parliament, held in the twentieth year of King Richard's reign.

NYMPHIDIA,

THE COURT OF FAIRY.

OLD Chaucer doth of Topas tell,
Mad Rabelais of Pantágruél,
A later third of Dowsabel,
    With such poor trifles playing;
Others the like have laboured at,
Some of this thing and some of that,
And many of they knew not what,
    But what they may be saying.

Another sort there be, that will
Be talking of the Fairies still,
For never can they have their fill,
    As they were wedded to them;
No tales of them their thirst can slake,
So much delight therein they take,
And some strange thing they fain would make,
    Knew they the way to do them.

Then since no Muse hath been so bold,
Or of the later, or the old,
Those elvish secrets to unfold,
    Which lie from others' reading;
My active Muse to light shall bring
The Court of that proud Fairy King,
And tell there of the revelling.
    Jove prosper my proceeding!

And thou, Nymphidia, gentle Fay,
Which, meeting me upon the way,
These secrets didst to me bewray,
    Which now I am in telling;
My pretty, light, fantastic maid,
I here invoke thee to my aid,
That I may speak what thou hast said,
    In numbers smoothly swelling.

This palace standeth in the air,
By necromancy placéd there,
That it no tempest needs to fear,
    Which way soe'er it blow it.
And somewhat southward tow'rds the noon,
Whence lies a way up to the moon,
And thence the Fairy can as soon
    Pass to the earth below it.

The walls of spiders' legs are made
Well mortiséd and finely laid;
It was the master of his trade
    It curiously that builded;
The windows of the eyes of cats,
And for the roof, instead of slats,
Is covered with the skins of bats,
    With moonshine that are gilded.

Hence Obe on him sport to make,
Their rest when weary mortals take,
And none but only fairies wake,
    Descendeth for his pleasure;
And Mab, his merry Queen, by night
Bestrides young folks that lie upright,
(In elder times the mare that hight,)
    Which plagues them out of measure.

Hence shadows, seeming idle shapes,
Of little frisking elves and apes
To earth do make their wanton scapes,
    As hope of pastime hastes them ;
Which maids think on the hearth they see
When fires well-nigh consuméd be,
There dancing hays by two and three,
    Just as their fancy casts them.

These make our girls their sluttery rue,
By pinching them both black and blue,
And put a penny in their shoe
    The house for cleanly sweeping ;
And in their courses make that round
In meadows and in marshes found,
Of them so called the Fairy Ground,
    Of which they have the keeping.

These when a child haps to be got
Which after proves an idiot
When folk perceive it thriveth not,
    The fault therein to smother,
Some silly, doting, brainless calf
That understands things by the half,
Say that the Fairy left this oaf
    And took away the other.

But listen, and I shall you tell
A chance in Faëry that befell,
Which certainly may please some well
    In love and arms delighting,
Of Oberon that jealous grew
Of one of his own Fairy crew,
Too well, he feared, his Queen that knew,
    His love but ill requiting.

Pigwiggin was this Fairy Knight,
One wondrous gracious in the sight
Of fair Queen Mab, which day and night
    He amorously observéd;
Which made King Oberon suspect
His service took too good effect,
His sauciness had often checkt,
    And could have wished him stervéd.

Pigwiggin gladly would commend
Some token to Queen Mab to send,
If sea or land him aught could lend
    Were worthy of her wearing;
At length this lover doth devise
A bracelet made of emmet's eyes,
A thing he thought that she would prize,
    No whit her state impairing.

And to the Queen a letter writes,
Which he most curiously indites,
Conjuring her by all the rites
    Of love, she would be pleaséd
To meet him, her true servant, where
They might, without suspect or fear,
Themselves to one another clear
    And have their poor hearts easéd.

At midnight, the appointed hour;
"And for the Queen a fitting bower,"
Qouth he, " is that fair cowslip flower
    On Hient hill that bloweth:
In all your train there's not a fay
That ever went to gather may
But she hath made it, in her way,
    The tallest there that groweth."

When by Tom Thumb, a Fairy Page,
He sent it, and doth him engage
By promise of a mighty wage
    It secretly to carry;
Which done, the Queen her maids doth call,
And bids them to be ready all:
She would go see her summer hall,
    She could no longer tarry.

Her chariot ready straight is made,
Each thing therein is fitting laid,
That she by nothing might be stayed,
    For nought must be her letting;
Four nimble gnats the horses were,
Their harnesses of gossamere,
Fly Cranion the charioteer
    Upon the coach-box getting.

Her chariot of a snail's fine shell,
Which for the colours did excel,
The fair Queen Mab becoming well,
    So lively was the limning;
The seat the soft wool of the bee,
The cover, gallantly to see,
The wing of a pied butterfly;
    I trow 'twas simple trimming.

The wheels composed of cricket's bones,
And daintily made for the nonce,
For fear of rattling on the stones
    With thistle-down they shod it;
For all her maidens much did fear
If Oberon had chance to hear
That Mab his Queen should have been there,
    He would not have abode it,

She mounts her chariot with a trice,
Nor would she stay, for no advice,
Until her maids that were so nice
    To wait on her were fitted ;
But ran herself away alone,
Which when they heard, there was not one
But hasted after to be gone,
    As he had been diswitted.

Hop and Mop and Drop so clear,
Pip and Trip and Skip that were
To Mab, their sovereign, ever dear,
    Her special maids of honour ;
Fib and Tib and Pink and Pin,
Tick and Quick and Jill and Jin,
Tit and Nit and Wap and Win,
    The train that wait upon her.

Upon a grasshopper they got
And, what with amble what with trot,
For hedge and ditch they sparéd not,
    But after her they hie them ;
A cobweb over them they throw,
To shield the wind if it should blow,
Themselves they wisely could bestow
    Lest any should espy them.

But let us leave Queen Mab a while,
Through many a gate, o'er many a stile,
That now had gotten by this wile,
    Her dear Pigwiggin kissing ;
And tell how Oberon doth fare,
Who grew as mad as any hare
When he had sought each place with care,
    And found his Queen was missing.

By grisly Pluto he doth swear,
He rent his clothes and tore his hair,
And as he runneth here and there
    An acorn cup he greeteth,
Which soon he taketh by the stalk,
About his head he lets it walk,
Nor doth he any creature balk,
    But lays on all he meeteth.

The Tuscan Poet doth advance
The frantic Paladin of France,
And those more ancient do enhance
    Alcides in his fury,
And others Aiax Telamon,
But to this time there hath been none
So Bedlam as our Oberon,
    Of which I dare assure ye.

And first encountering with a Wasp,
He in his arms the fly doth clasp
As though his breath he forth would grasp,
    Him for Pigwiggin taking:
"Where is my wife, thou rogue?" quoth he;
"Pigwiggin, she is come to thee;
Restore her, or thou diest by me!"
    Whereat the poor Wasp quaking

Cries, "Oberon, great Fairy King,
Content thee, I am no such thing:
I am a Wasp, behold my sting!"
    At which the Fairy started;
When soon away the Wasp doth go,
Poor wretch, was never frighted so;
He thought his wings were much too slow,
    O'erjoyed they so were parted.

He next upon a Glow-worm light,
You must suppose it now was night,
Which, for her hinder part was bright,
    He took to be a devil,
And furiously doth her assail
For carrying fire in her tail;
He thrashed her rough coat with his flail;
    The mad King feared no evil.

"Oh!" quoth the Glow-worm, "hold thy hand,
Thou puissant King of Fairy-land!
Thy mighty strokes who may withstand?
    Hold, or of life despair I!"
Together then herself doth roll,
And tumbling down into a hole
She seemed as black as any coal;
    Which vext away the Fairy.

From thence he ran into a hive:
Amongst the bees he letteth drive,
And down their combs begins to rive,
    All likely to have spoiléd,
Which with their wax his face besmeared,
And with their honey daubed his beard:
It would have made a man afeared
    To see how he was moiléd.

A new adventure him betides;
He met an Ant, which he bestrides,
And post thereon away he rides,
    Which with his haste doth stumble;
And came full over on her snout,
Her heels so threw the dirt about,
For she by no means could get out,
    But over him doth tumble.

And being in this piteous case,
And all be-slurréd head and face,
On runs he in this wild-goose chase,
　　As here and there he rambles ;
Half blind, against a molehole hit,
And for a mountain taking it,
For all he was out of his wit
　　Yet to the top he scrambles.

And being gotten to the top,
Yet there himself he could not stop,
But down on the other side doth chop,
　　And to the foot came rumbling ;
So that the grubs, therein that bred,
Hearing such turmoil overhead,
Thought surely they had all been dead ;
　　So fearful was the jumbling.

And falling down into a lake,
Which him up to the neck doth take,
His fury somewhat it doth slake ;
　　He calleth for a ferry ;
Where you may some recovery note :
What was his club he made his boat,
And in his oaken cup doth float,
　　As safe as in a wherry.

Men talk of the adventures strange
Of Don Quixote, and of their change
Through which he arméd oft did range,
　　Of Sancho Pancha's travel ;
But should a man tell everything
Done by this frantic Fairy King,
And them in lofty numbers sing,
　　It well his wits might gravel.

Scarce set on shore, but therewithal
He meeteth Puck, which most men call
Hobgoblin, and on him doth fall,
    With words from frenzy spoken :
"Oh, oh," quoth Hob, "God save thy grace!
Who drest thee in this piteous case?
He thus that spoiled my sovereign's face,
    I would his neck were broken!"

This Puck seems but a dreaming dolt,
Still walking like a ragged colt,
And oft out of a bush doth bolt,
    Of purpose to deceive us ;
And leading us makes us to stray,
Long winter's nights, out of the way;
And when we stick in mire and clay,
    Hob doth with laughter leave us.

"Dear Puck," quoth he, "my wife is gone:
As e'er thou lov'st King Oberon,
Let everything but this alone,
    With vengeance and pursue her ;
Bring her to me alive or dead,
Or that vile thief, Pigwiggin's head,
That villain hath [my Queen misled] ;
    He to this folly drew her."

Quoth Puck, "My liege, I'll never lin,
But I will through thick and thin,
Until at length I bring her in ;
    My dearest lord, ne'er doubt it."
Through brake, through briar,
Through muck, through mire,
Through water, through fire ;
    And thus goes Puck about it.

This thing Nymphidia overheard,
That on this mad king had a guard,
Not doubting of a great reward,
    For first this business broaching;
And through the air away doth go,
Swift as an arrow from the bow,
To let her sovereign Mab to know
    What peril was approaching.

The Queen bound with Love's powerful charm
Sate with Pigwiggin arm in arm;
Her merry maids, that thought no harm,
    About the room were skipping;
A humble-bee, their minstrel, played
Upon his hautboy, every maid
Fit for this revel was arrayed,
    The hornpipe neatly tripping.

In comes Nymphidia, and doth cry,
" My sovereign, for your safety fly,
For there is danger but too nigh;
    I posted to forewarn you:
The King hath sent Hobgoblin out,
To seek you all the fields about,
And of your safety you may doubt,
    If he but once discern you."

When, like an uproar in a town
Before them everything went down;
Some tore a ruff, and some a gown,
    'Gainst one another justling;
They flew about like chaff i' th' wind;
For haste some left their masks behind;
Some could not stay their gloves to find;
    There never was such bustling.

Forth ran they, by a secret way,
Into a brake that near them lay;
Yet much they doubted there to stay,
　　Lest Hob should hap to find them;
He had a sharp and piercing sight,
All one to him the day and night;
And therefore were resolved, by flight,
　　To leave this place behind them.

At length one chanced to find a nut,
In the end of which a hole was cut,
Which lay upon a hazel root,
　　There scattered by a squirrel
Which out the kernel gotten had;
When quoth this Fay, "Dear Queen, be glad;
Let Oberon be ne'er so mad,
　　I'll set you safe from peril.

"Come all into this nut," quoth she,
"Come closely in; be ruled by me;
Each one may here a chooser be,
　　For room ye need not wrastle:
Nor need ye be together heaped;"
So one by one therein they crept,
And lying down they soundly slept,
　　And safe as in a castle.

Nymphidia, that this while doth watch,
Perceived if Puck the Queen should catch
That he should be her over-match,
　　Of which she well bethought her;
Found it must be some powerful charm,
The Queen against him that must arm,
Or surely he would do her harm,
　　For throughly he had sought her.

And listening if she aught could hear,
That her might hinder, or might fear;
But finding still the coast was clear;
    Nor creature had descried her;
Each circumstance and having scanned,
She came thereby to understand,
Puck would be with them out of hand;
    When to her charms she hied her.

And first her fern-seed doth bestow,
The kernel of the mistletoe;
And here and there as Puck should go,
    With terror to affright him,
She night-shade strews to work him ill,
Therewith her vervain and her dill,
That hindereth witches of their will,
    Of purpose to despite him.

Then sprinkles she the juice of rue,
That groweth underneath the yew;
With nine drops of the midnight dew,
    From lunary distilling:
The molewarp's brain mixed therewithal;
And with the same the pismire's gall:
For she in nothing short would fall,
    The Fairy was so willing.

Then thrice under a briar doth creep,
Which at both ends was rooted deep,
And over it three times she leap;
    Her magic much availing:
Then on Prosérpina doth call,
And so upon her spell doth fall,
Which here to you repeat I shall,
    Not in one tittle failing.

"By the croaking of a frog;
By the howling of the dog;
By the crying of the hog
　　Against the storm arising;
By the evening curfew bell,
By the doleful dying knell,
O let this my direful spell,
　　Hob, hinder my surprising!

"By the mandrake's dreadful groans;
By the lubrican's sad moans;
By the noise of dead men's bones
　　In charnel-houses rattling;
By the hissing of the snake,
The rustling of the fire-drake,
I charge the thou this place forsake,
　　Nor of Queen Mab be prattling!

"By the whirlwind's hollow sound,
By the thunder's dreadful stound,
Yells of spirits underground,
　　I charge thee not to fear us;
By the screech-owl's dismal note,
By the black night-raven's throat,
I charge thee, Hob, to tear thy coat
　　With thorns, if thou come near us!"

Her spell thus spoke, she stept aside,
And in a chink herself doth hide,
To see thereof what would betide,
　　For she doth only mind him:
When presently she Puck espies,
And well she marked his gloating eyes,
How under every leaf he pries,
　　In seeking still to find them.

But once the circle got within,
The charms to work do straight begin,
And he was caught as in a gin ;
    For as he thus was busy,
A pain he in his head-piece feels,
Against a stubbéd tree he reels,
And up went poor Hobgoblin's heels,
    Alas! his brain was dizzy!

At length upon his feet he gets,
Hobgoblin fumes, Hobgoblin frets;
And as again he forward sets,
    And through the bushes scrambles,
A stump doth trip him in his pace ;
Down comes poor Hob upon his face,
And lamentably tore his case,
    Amongst the briars and brambles.

"A plague upon Queen Mab!" quoth he,
"And all her maids where'er they be:
I think the devil guided me,
    To seekèd her so provokéd!"
Where stumbling at a piece of wood,
He fell into a ditch of mud,
Where to the very chin he stood,
    In danger to be chokéd.

Now worse than e'er he was before,
Poor Puck doth yell, poor Puck doth roar,
That waked Queen Mab, who doubted sore
    Some treason had been wrought her :
Until Nymphidia told the Queen,
What she had done, what she had seen,
Who then had well near cracked her spleen
    With very extreme laughter.

But leave we Hob to clamber out,
Queen Mab and all her Fairy rout,
And come again to have a bout
    With Oberon yet madding :
And with Pigwiggin now distraught,
Who much was troubled in his thought,
That he so long the Queen had sought,
    And through the fields was gadding.

And as he runs he still doth cry,
" King Oberon, I thee defy,
And dare thee here in arms to try,
    For my dear lady's honour :
For that she is a Queen right good,
In whose defence I'll shed my blood,
And that thou in this jealous mood
    Hast laid this slander on her."

And quickly arms him for the field,
A little cockle-shell his shield,
Which he could very bravely wield ;
    Yet could it not be percéd :
His spear a bent both stiff and strong,
And well near of two inches long :
The pile was of a horse-fly's tongue,
    Whose sharpness nought reverséd.

And puts him on a coat of mail,
Which was of a fish's scale,
That when his foe should him assail,
    No point should be prevailing :
His rapier was a hornet's sting ;
It was a very dangerous thing,
For if he chanced to hurt the King,
    It would be long in healing.

His helmet was a beetle's head,
Most horrible and full of dread,
That able was to strike one dead,
    Yet did it well become him ;
And for a plume a horse's hair
Which, being tosséd with the air,
Had force to strike his foe with fear,
    And turn his weapon from him.

Himself he on an earwig set,
Yet scarce he on his back could get,
So oft and high he did curvét,
    Ere he himself could settle :
He made him turn, and stop, and bound,
To gallop and to trot the round,
He scarce could stand on any ground,
    He was so full of mettle.

When soon he met with Tomalin,
One that a valiant knight had been,
And to King Oberon of kin ;
    Quoth he, "Thou manly Fairy,
Tell Oberon I come prepared,
Then bid him stand upon his guard ;
This hand his baseness shall reward,
    Let him be ne'er so wary.

"Say to him thus, that I defy
His slanders and his infamy,
And as a mortal enemy
    Do publicly proclaim him :
Withal that if I had mine own,
He should not wear the Fairy crown,
But with a vengeance should come down,
    Nor we a king should name him."

This Tomalin could not abide,
To hear his sovereign vilified;
But to the Fairy Court him hied,
   (Full furiously he posted,)
With everything Pigwiggin said:
How title to the crown he laid,
And in what arms he was arrayed,
   As how himself he boasted.

'Twixt head and foot, from point to point,
He told the arming of each joint,
In every piece how neat and quoint,
   For Tomalin could do it:
How fair he sat, how sure he rid,
As of the courser he bestrid,
How managed, and how well he did;
   The King which listened to it,

Quoth he, " Go, Tomalin, with speed,
Provide me arms, provide my steed,
And everything that I shall need;
   By thee I will be guided;
To straight account call thou thy wit;
See there be wanting not a whit,
In everything see thou me fit,
   Just as my foe's provided."

Soon flew this news through Fairy-land,
Which gave Queen Mab to understand
The combat that was then in hand
   Betwixt those men so mighty:
Which greatly she began to rue,
Perceiving that all Fairy knew
The first occasion from her grew
   Of these affairs so weighty.

Wherefore attended with her maids,
Through fogs, and mists, and damps she wades,
To Proserpine the Queen of Shades,
    To treat, that it would please her
The cause into her hands to take,
For ancient love and friendship's sake,
And soon thereof an end to make,
    Which of much care would ease her.

A while there let we Mab alone,
And come we to King Oberon,
Who, armed to meet his foe, is gone,
    For proud Pigwiggin crying:
Who sought the Fairy King as fast,
And had so well his journeys cast,
That he arrivéd at the last,
    His puissant foe espying.

Stout Tomalin came with the King,
Tom Thumb doth on Pigwiggin bring,
That perfect were in everything
    To single fights belonging:
And therefore they themselves engage,
To see them exercise their rage,
With fair and comely equipage,
    Not one the other wronging.

So like in arms these champions were,
As they had been a very pair,
So that a man would almost swear
    That either had been either;
Their furious steeds began to neigh,
That they were heard a mighty way;
Their staves upon their rests they lay;
    Yet ere they flew together

Their seconds minister an oath,
Which was indifferent to them both,
That on their knightly faith and troth
    No magic them suppliéd ;
And sought them that they had no charms,
Wherewith to work each other harms,
But came with simple open arms
    To have their causes triéd.

Together furiously they ran,
That to the ground came horse and man,
The blood out of their helmets span,
    So sharp were their encounters ;
And though they to the earth were thrown,
Yet quickly they regained their own,
Such nimbleness was never shown,
    They were two gallant mounters.

When in a second course again,
They forward came with might and main,
Yet which had better of the twain,
    The seconds could not judge yet ;
Their shields were into pieces cleft,
Their helmets from their heads were reft,
And to defend them nothing left,
    These champions would not budge yet.

Away from them their staves they threw,
Their cruel swords they quickly drew,
And freshly they the fight renew,
    They every stroke redoubled ;
Which made Prosérpina take heed,
And make to them the greater speed,
For fear lest they too much should bleed,
    Which wondrously her troubled.

When to the infernal Styx she goes,
She takes the fogs from thence that rose,
And in a bag doth them enclose:
  When well she had them blended.
She hies her then to Lethe spring,
A bottle and thereof doth bring,
Wherewith she meant to work the thing
  Which only she intended.

Now Proserpine with Mab is gone,
Unto the place where Oberon
And proud Pigwiggin, one to one,
  Both to be slain were likely:
And there themselves they closely hide,
Because they would not be espied;
For Proserpine meant to decide
  The matter very quickly.

And suddenly unties the poke,
Which out of it sent such a smoke,
As ready was them all to choke,
  So grievous was the pother;
So that the knights each other lost,
And stood as still as any post;
Tom Thumb nor Tomalin could boast
  Themselves of any other.

But when the mist 'gan somewhat cease;
Prosérpina commandeth peace;
And that a while they should release
  Each other of their peril:
"Which here," quoth she, "I do proclaim
To all in dreadful Pluto's name,
That as ye will eschew his blame,
  You let me hear the quarrel:

"But here yourselves you must engage,
Somewhat to cool your spleenish rage;
Your grievous thirst and to assuage
    That first you drink this liquor,
Which shall your understanding clear,
As plainly shall to you appear;
Those things from me that you shall hear,
    Conceiving much the quicker."

This Lethe water, you must know,
The memory destroyeth so,
That of our weal, or of our woe,
    Is all remembrance blotted,
Of it nor can you ever think;
For they no sooner took this drink,
But nought into their brains could sink
    Of what had them besotted.

King Oberon forgotten had
That he for jealousy ran mad,
But of his Queen was wondrous glad,
    And asked how they came thither:
Pigwiggin likewise doth forget
That he Queen Mab had ever met,
Or that they were so hard beset,
    When they were found together.

Nor neither of them both had thought
That e'er they each had other sought,
Much less that they a combat fought,
    But such a dream were lothing.
Tom Thumb had got a little sup,
And Tomalin scarce kissed the cup,
Yet had their brains so sure locked up,
    That they remembered nothing.

Queen Mab and her light maids, the while,
Amongst themselves do closely smile,
To see the King caught with this wile,
　With one another jesting :
And to the Fairy Court they went,
With mickle joy and merriment,
Which thing was done with good intent,
　And thus I left them feasting.

IDEA.

I.

LIKE an adventurous seafarer am I,
Who hath some long and dangerous voyage been,
And called to tell of his discovery,
How far he sailed, what countries he had seen,
Proceeding from the port whence he put forth,
Shows by his compass how his course he steered ;
When east, when west, when south, and when by north,
As how the pole to every place was reared,
What capes he doubled, of what continent,
The gulfs and straits that strangely he had passed,
Where most becalmèd, where with foul breath spent,
And on what rocks in peril to be cast :
  Thus in my love, time calls me to relate
  My tedious travels and oft varying fate.

2.

MY heart was slain, and none but you and I ;
Who should I think the murder should commit ?
Since but yourself there was no creature by,
But only I, guiltless of murdering it.
It slew itself; the verdict on the view
Do quit the dead, and me not accessory :
Well, well, I fear it will be proved, by you
The evidence so great a proof doth carry.
But O, see, see, we need enquire no further,
Upon your lips the scarlet drops are found,
And in your eye the boy that did the murther,
Your cheeks yet pale, since first he gave the wound.
  By this I see, however things be past,
  Yet Heaven will still have murder out at last.

3.

TAKING my pen, with words to cast my woe,
Duly to count the sum of all my cares,
I find my griefs innumerable grow,
The reckonings rise to millions of despairs ;
And thus, dividing of my fatal hours,
The payments of my love I read and cross ;
Subtracting, set my sweets unto my sours,
My joy's arrearage leads me to my loss :
And thus, mine eyes a debtor to thine eye
Which by extortion gaineth all their looks,
My heart hath paid such grievous usury,
That all their wealth lies in thy beauty's books ;
  And all is thine which hath been due to me,
  And I a bankrupt, quite undone by thee.

4.

BRIGHT star of beauty, on whose eyelids sit
A thousand nymph-like and enamoured graces,
The goddesses of Memory and Wit
Which there in order take their several places;
In whose dear bosom sweet delicious Love
Lays down his quiver, which he once did bear,
Since he that blessèd Paradise did prove,
And leaves his mother's lap to sport him there:
Let others strive to entertain with words,
My soul is of a braver metal made;
I hold that vile which vulgar wit affords;
In me's that faith which time cannot invade.
    Let what I praise be still made good by you:
    Be you most worthy whilst I am most true.

5.

NOTHING but No and I, and I and No: [I=aye.]
How falls it out so strangely you reply?
I tell you, fair, I'll not be answered so,
With this affirming No, denying I.
I say, I love, you slightly answer I:
I say, you love, you pule me out a No:
I say, I die, you echo me with I:
Save me! I cry, you sigh me out a No.
Must woe and I have nought but No and I?
No I, am I, if I no more can have;
Answer no more, with silence make reply,
And let me take myself what I do crave:
    Let No and I with I and you be so:
    Then answer No and I, and I and No.

6.

HOW many paltry, foolish, painted things
That now in coaches trouble every street,
Shall be forgotten, whom no poet sings,
Ere they be well wrapped in their winding-sheet ?
Where I to thee eternity shall give
When nothing else remaineth of these days,
And Queens hereafter shall be glad to live
Upon the alms of thy superfluous praise.
Virgins and matrons reading these my rhymes,
Shall be so much delighted with thy story,
That they shall grieve they lived not in these times,
To have seen thee, their sex's only glory :
   So shalt thou fly above the vulgar throng,
   Still to survive in my immortal song.

7.

LOVE in a humour played the prodigal,
And bade my senses to a solemn feast ;
Yet more to grace the company withal,
Invites my heart to be the chiefest guest :
No other drink would serve this glutton's turn
But precious tears distilling from mine eyne,
Which with my sighs this epicure doth burn,
Quaffing carouses in this costly wine ;
Where, in his cups o'ercome with foul excess,
Straightways he plays a swaggering ruffian's part,
And at the banquet in his drunkenness
Slew his dear friend, my kind and truest heart ;
   A gentle warning, friends, thus may you see,
   What 'tis to keep a drunkard company.

8.

THERE'S nothing grieves me but that age should haste,
That in my days I may not see thee old,
That where those two clear sparkling eyes are placed,
Only two loopholes then I might behold.
That lovely archéd, ivory polished brow,
Defaced with wrinkles that I might but see ;
Thy dainty hair, so curled and crispéd now,
Like grizzled moss upon some aged tree ;
Thy cheek, now flush with roses, sunk and lean,
Thy lips, with age, as any wafer thin,
Thy pearly teeth out of thy head so clean,
That when thou feedest thy nose shall touch thy chin :
   These lines that now thou scorn'st, which should delight thee,
   Then would I make thee read but to despite thee.

9.

AS other men, so I myself do muse
Why in this sort I wrest invention so,
And why these giddy metaphors I use,
Leaving the path the greater part do go ;
I will resolve you : I am lunatic,
And ever this in madmen you shall find,
What they last thought of when the brain grew sick,
In most distraction they keep that in mind.
Thus talking idly in this bedlam fit,
Reason and I, you must conceive, are twain,
'Tis nine years now since first I lost my wit,
Bear with me then, though troubled be my brain :
   With diet and correction men distraught,
   Not too far past, may to their wits be brought.

10.

To nothing fitter can I thee compare
Than to the son of some rich penny-father,
Who having now brought on his end with care,
Leaves to his son all he had heaped together;
This new rich novice, lavish of his chest,
To one man gives, doth on another spend,
Then here he riots, yet amongst the rest
Haps to lend some to one true honest friend.
Thy gifts thou in obscurity dost waste,
False friends thy kindness, born but to deceive thee;
Thy love, that is on the unworthy placed,
Time hath thy beauty, which with age will leave thee;
    Only that little which to me was lent
    I give thee back when all the rest is spent.

11.

You not alone, when you are still alone,
O God, from you that I could private be,
Since you one were, I never since was one,
Since you in me, myself since out of me,
Transported from myself into your being,
Though either distant, present yet to either,
Senseless with too much joy, each other seeing,
And only absent when we are together.
Give me myself, and take yourself again,
Devise some means but how I may forsake you,
So much is mine that doth with you remain,
That taking what is mine, with me I take you;
    You do bewitch me, O that I could fly
    From myself you, or from your own self I.

12.
TO THE SOUL.

THAT learnéd Father, who so firmly proves
The soul of man immortal and divine,
And doth the several offices define,
Anima, Gives her that name, as she the body moves,
Amor, Then is she love, embracing charity,
Animus, Moving a will in us, it is the mind,
Mens, Retaining knowledge, still the same in kind,
Memoria, As intellectual, it is memory,
Ratio, In judging, Reason only is her name,
Sensus, In speedy apprehension it is sense,
Conscientia, In right or wrong they call her Conscience,
Spiritus, The spirit, when it to Godward doth inflame;
    These of the soul the several functions be,
    Which my heart, lightened by thy love, doth see.

13.
TO THE SHADOW.

LETTERS and lines we see are soon defaced,
Metals do waste and fret with canker's rust,
The diamond shall once consume to dust,
And freshest colours with foul stains disgraced;
Paper and ink can paint but naked words,
To write with blood of force offends the sight,
And if with tears I find them all too light,
And sighs and signs a silly hope affords.
O sweetest Shadow, how thou serv'st my turn!
Which still shalt be, as long as there is sun;
Nor whilst the world is, never shall be done,
Whilst moon shall shine or any fire shall burn;
    That everything whence Shadow doth proceed,
    May in his shadow my love's story read.

14.

IF he from Heaven that filched that living fire
Condemned by Jove to endless torment be,
I greatly marvel how you still go free
That far beyond Prometheus did aspire:
The fire he stole, although of heavenly kind,
Which from above he craftily did take,
Of lifeless clods us living men to make,
He did bestow in temper of the mind:
But you broke into Heaven's immortal store,
Where virtue, honour, wit, and beauty lay;
Which taking thence you have escaped away,
Yet stand as free as e'er you did before;
   Yet old Prometheus punished for his rape:
   Thus poor thieves suffer when the greater scape.

15.

HIS REMEDY FOR LOVE.

SINCE to obtain thee nothing we will stead,
I have a medicine that shall cure my love,
The powder of her heart, dried when she's dead,
That gold nor honour ne'er had power to move;
Mixed with her tears that ne'er her true love crost,
Nor at fifteen ne'er longed to be a bride;
Boiled with her sighs, in giving up the ghost,
That for her late deceaséd husband died;
Into the same then let a woman breathe
That being chid did never word reply;
With one thrice married's prayers that did bequeath
A legacy to stale virginity;
   If this receipt have not the power to win me,
   Little I'll say, but think the devil's in me.

16.
AN ALLUSION TO THE PHŒNIX.

'MONGST all the creatures in this spacious round,
Of the bird kind, the Phœnix is alone,
Which best by you of living things is known;
None like to that, none like to you is found.
Your beauty is the hot and splendrous sun,
The precious spices be your chaste desire,
Which being kindled by that heavenly fire,
Your life so like the Phœnix's begun;
Yourself thus burnéd in that sacred flame,
With so rare sweetness all the heavens perfuming,
Again increasing as you are consuming,
Only by dying born the very same;
    And winged by fame you to the stars ascend,
    So you of time shall live beyond the end.

17.
TO TIME.

STAY, speedy Time, behold before thou pass,
From age to age what thou hast sought to see,
One in whom all the excellences be,
In whom Heaven looks itself as in a glass;
Time, look thou too in this translucent glass,
And thy youth past in this pure mirror see,
As the world's beauty in his infancy,
What it was then, and thou before it was.
Pass on, and to posterity tell this,
Yet see thou tell but truly what hath been,
Say to our nephews that thou once hast seen
In perfect human shape all heavenly bliss;
    And bid them mourn, nay more, despair with thee,
    That she is gone, her like again to see.

18.
TO THE CELESTIAL NUMBERS.

To this our world, to learning and to Heaven,
Three Nines there are, to every one a nine,
One number of the earth, the other both divine;
One woman now makes three odd numbers even.
Nine orders first of angels be in Heaven,
Nine Muses do with learning still frequent,
These with the gods are ever resident.
Nine worthy women to the world were given:
My worthy one to these nine worthies addeth,
And my fair Muse, one Muse unto the nine,
And my good angel, in my soul divine,
With one more order these nine orders gladdeth;
   My Muse, my worthy, and my angel then,
   Makes every one of these three nines a ten.

19.
TO HUMOUR.

You cannot love, my pretty heart, and why?
There was a time you told me that you would:
But now again you will the same deny,
If it might please you, would to God you could.
What, will you hate? nay, that you will not neither;
Nor love, nor hate, how then? what will you do?
What, will you keep a mean then betwixt either?
Or will you love me, and yet hate me too?
Yet serves not this: what next, what other shift?
You will and will not, what a coil is here.
I see your craft now I perceive your drift,
And all this while I was mistaken there;
   Your love and hate is this, I now do prove you,
   You love in hate, by hate to make me love you.

20.

An evil spirit, your beauty, haunts me still,
Wherewith, alas, I have been long possest,
Which ceaseth not to tempt me to each ill,
Nor gives me once but one poor minute's rest ;
In me it speaks, whether I sleep or wake,
And when by means to drive it out I try,
With greater torments than it me doth take,
And tortures me in most extremity ;
Before my face it lays down my despairs,
And hastes me on unto a sudden death ;
Now tempting me to drown myself in tears,
And then in sighing to give up my breath :
 Thus am I still provoked to every evil,
 By this good wicked spirit, sweet angel devil.

21.

A witless gallant a young wench that wooed
(Yet his dull spirit her not one jot could move)
Entreated me, as e'er I wished his good,
To write him but one sonnet to his love :
When I, as fast as e'er my pen could trot,
Poured out what first from quick invention came ;
Nor never stood one word thereof to blot,
Much like his wit that was to use the same ;
But with my verses he his mistress won,
Who doted on the dolt beyond all measure,
But see, for you to Heaven for phrase I run,
And ransacked all Apollo's golden treasure ;
 Yet by my froth this fool his love obtains,
 And I lose you for all my wit and pains.

22.
TO FOLLY.

WITH fools and children good discretion bears,
Then, honest people, bear with love and me,
Nor older yet, nor wiser made by years,
Amongst the rest of fools and children be :
Love, still a baby, plays with gawds and toys,
And like a wanton sports with every feather ;
And idiots still are running after boys,
Then fools and children fittest to go together :
He still as young as when he first was born,
No wiser I than when as young as he.
You that behold us, laugh us not to scorn,
Give Nature thanks, ye are not such as we :
    Yet fools and children sometimes tell in play,
    Some wise in show more fools indeed than they.

23.

LOVE, banished Heaven, in earth was held in scorn,
Wandering abroad in need and beggary ;
And wanting friends, though of a goddess born,
Yet craved the alms of such as passéd by :
I, like a man devout and charitable,
Clothéd the naked, lodged this wandering guest,
With sighs and tears still furnishing his table,
With what might make the miserable blest ;
But this ungrateful, for my good desert,
Enticed my thoughts against me to conspire,
Who gave consent to steal away my heart,
And set my breast, his lodging, on a fire. [bold,
    Well, well, my friends, when beggars grow thus
    No marvel then though charity grow cold,

24.

I HEAR some say, "This man is not in love:
Who? can he love? a likely thing," they say;
"Read but his verse, and it will easily prove."
O, judge not rashly, gentle Sir, I pray,
Because I loosely trifle in this sort,
As one that fain his sorrows would beguile:
You now suppose me all this time in sport,
And please yourself with this conceit the while.
Ye shallow censures, sometimes see ye not
In greatest perils some men pleasant be,
Where fame by death is only to be got,
They resolute? So stands the case with me;
  Where other men in depth of passion cry,
  I laugh at Fortune, as in jest to die.

25.

OH, why should Nature niggardly restrain
That foreign nations relish not our tongue!
Else should my lines glide on the waves of Rhine,
And crown the Pyrens with my living song:
But bounded thus, to Scotland get you forth,
Thence take you wing unto the Orcades,
There let my verse get glory in the North,
Making my sighs to thaw the frozen seas:
And let the bards within that Irish isle,
To whom my Muse with fiery wings shall pass,
Call back the stiffnecked rebels from exile,
And mollify the slaughtering galliglass;
  And when my flowing numbers they rehearse,
  Let wolves and bears be charmèd with my verse.

26.
TO DESPAIR.

I EVER love, where never hope appears,
Yet hope draws on my never hoping care,
And my life's hope would die but for despair.
My never certain joy breeds ever certain fears,
Uncertain dread gives wings unto my hope;
Yet my hope's wings are laden so with fear
As they cannot ascend to my hope's sphere;
Though fear gives them more than a heavenly scope
Yet this large room is bounded with despair,
So my love still is fettered with vain hope,
And liberty deprives him of his scope,
And thus am I imprisoned in the air:
  Then, sweet Despair, a while hold up thy head,
  Or all my hope for sorrow will be dead.

27.

Is not love here, as 'tis in other climes,
And differeth it as do the several nations?
Or hath it lost the virtue with the times,
Or in this island altereth with the fashions?
Or have our passions lesser power than theirs
Who had less art them lively to express?
Is Nature grown less powerful in their heirs,
Or in our fathers did she more transgress?
I'm sure my sighs come from a heart as true
As any man's that memory can boast,
And my respects and services to you -
Equal with his that loves his mistress most:
  Or Nature must be partial in my cause,
  Or only you do violate her laws.

28.

To such as say thy love I over-prize,
And do not stick to term my praises folly;
Against these folk, that think themselves so wise,
I thus oppose my reason's forces wholly:
Though I give more than well affords my state,
In which expense the most suppose me vain,
Which yields them nothing at the easiest rate,
Yet at this price returns me treble gain.
They value not, unskilful how to use,
And I give much, because I gain thereby:
I that thus take, or they that thus refuse,
Whether are these deceivéd then, or I?
   In everything I hold this maxim still,
   The circumstance doth make it good or ill.

29.
TO THE SENSES.

WHEN conquering love did first my heart assail,
Unto mine aid I summoned every sense,
Doubting, if that proud tyrant should prevail,
My heart should suffer for mine eyes' offence;
But he with beauty first corrupted sight,
My hearing bribed with her tongue's harmony,
My taste by her sweet lips drawn with delight,
My smelling won with her breath's spicery:
But when my touching came to play his part
(The king of senses, greater than the rest),
He yields love up the keys unto my heart,
And tells the other how they should be blest:
   And thus by those of whom I hoped for aid,
   To cruel love my soul was first betrayed.

30.
TO THE VESTALS.

THOSE priests which first the vestal fire began,
Which might be borrowed from no earthly flame,
Devised a vessel to receive the sun,
Being steadfastly opposéd to the same;
Where, with sweet wood, laid curiously by art,
On which the sun might by reflection beat,
Receiving strength from every secret part,
The fuel kindled with celestial heat.
Thy blessed eyes, the sun which lights this fire,
My holy thoughts, they be the vestal flame,
The precious odours be my chaste desire,
My breasts the vessels which include the same:
   Thou art my Vesta, thou my goddess art,
   Thy hallowed temple only is my heart.

31.
TO THE CRITICS.

METHINKS I see some crooked mimic jeer,
And tax my Muse with this fantastic grace,
Turning my papers, asks, "What have we here?"
Making withal some filthy antic face.
I fear no censure, nor what thou canst say,
Nor shall my spirit one jot of vigour lose;
Thinkest thou my wit shall keep the pack-horse way
That every dudgeon low invention goes?
Since sonnets thus in bundles are imprest,
And every drudge doth dull our satiate ear;
Think'st thou my love shall in those rags be drest
That every dowdy, every trull doth wear?
   Up to my pitch no common judgment flies,
   I scorn all earthly dung-bred scarabies.

32.
TO THE RIVER ANKOR.

OUR floods' queen, Thames, for ships and swans is crowned,
And stately Severn for her shore is praised,
The crystal Trent for fords and fish renowned,
And Avon's fame to Albion's cliffs is raised,
Carlegion Chester vaunts her holy Dee,
York many wonders of her Ouse can tell;
The Peak her Dove, whose banks so fertile be,
And Kent will say her Medway doth excel;
Cotswold commends her Isis to the Tame,
Our Northern borders boast of Tweed's fair flood,
Our Western parts extol their Wilis fame,
And the old Lea brags of the Danish blood;
   Arden's sweet Ankor, let thy glory be,
   That fair Idea only lives by thee.

33.
TO IMAGINATION.

WHILST yet mine eyes do surfeit with delight,
My woful heart imprisoned in my breast,
Wisheth to be transforméd to my sight,
That it, like those, by looking might be blest:
But whilst mine eyes thus greedily do gaze,
Finding their objects over-soon depart,
These now the others' happiness do praise,
Wishing themselves that they had been my heart;
That eyes were heart, or that the heart were eyes,
As covetous the other's use to have:
But finding Nature their request denies,
This to each other mutually they crave:
   That since the one cannot the other be,
   That eyes could think of that my heart could see.

34.
TO ADMIRATION.

MARVEL not, love, though I thy power admire,
Ravished a world beyond the farthest thought,
And knowing more than ever hath been taught,
That I am only starved in my desire;
Marvel not, love, though I thy power admire,
Aiming at things exceeding all perfection,
To wisdom's self to minister direction,
That I am only starved in my desire;
Marvel not, love, though I thy power admire,
Though my conceit I further seem to bend
Than possibly invention can extend,
And yet am only starved in my desire:
   If thou wilt wonder, here's the wonder, love,
   That this to me doth yet no wonder prove.

35.
TO MIRACLE.

SOME, misbelieving and profane in love,
When I do speak of miracles by thee,
May say that thou art flatteréd by me,
Who only write my skill in verse to prove;
See miracles, ye unbelieving, see,
A dumb-born Muse made to express the mind,
A cripple hand to write, yet lame by kind,
One by thy name, the other touching thee;
Blind were mine eyes till they were seen of thine,
And mine ears deaf, by thy fame healéd be,
My vices cured by virtues sprung from thee,
My hopes revived, which long in grave had lain:
   All unclean thoughts foul spirits cast out in me,
   Only by virtue that proceeds from thee.

36.
CUPID CONJURED.

 THOU purblind boy, since thou hast been so slack
To wound her heart whose eyes have wounded me,
And suffered her to glory in my wrack,
Thus to my aid I lastly conjure thee;
By hellish Styx, by which the Thunderer swears,
By thy fair mother's unavoided power,
By Hecate's names, by Proserpine's sad tears,
When she was rapt to the infernal bower;
By thine own lovéd Psyche's, by the fires
Spent on thine altars, flaming up to Heaven;
By all true lover's sighs, vows, and desires,
By all the wounds that ever thou hast given,
   I conjure thee by all that I have named,
   To make her love, or, Cupid, be thou damned.

37.

DEAR, why should you command me to my rest,
When now the night doth summon all to sleep?
Methinks this time becometh lovers best;
Night was ordained together friends to keep:
How happy are all other living things,
Which though the day disjoin by several flight,
The quiet evening yet together brings,
And each returns unto his love at night?
O thou that art so courteous else to all!
Why shouldst thou, Night, abuse me only thus,
That every creature to his kind dost call,
And yet 'tis thou dost only sever us?
   Well could I wish it would be ever day,
   If, when night comes, you bid me go away.

38.

SITTING alone, Love bids me go and write;
Reason plucks back, commanding me to stay,
Boasting that she doth still direct the way,
Or else Love were unable to indite.
Love growing angry, vexéd at the spleen,
And scorning Reason's maiméd argument,
Straight taxeth Reason, wanting to invent,
Where she with Love conversing hath not been.
Reason, reproachéd with this coy disdain,
Despiteth Love, and laugheth at her folly;
And Love contemning Reason's reason wholly,
Thought it in weight too light by many a grain:
   Reason put back, doth out of sight remove,
   And Love alone picks reason out of love.

39.

SOME, when in rhyme they of their loves do tell,
With flames and lightnings their exordiums paint,
Some call on Heaven, some invocate on Hell,
And Fates and Furies with their woes acquaint.
Elysium is too high a seat for me,
I will not come in Styx or Phlegeton,
The thrice-three Muses but too wanton be,
Like they that lust, I care not, I will none.
Spiteful Erinnys frights me with her looks,
My manhood dares not with foul Até mell,
I quake to look on Hecate's charming books,
I still fear bugbears in Apollo's cell:
   I pass not for Minerva, nor Astrea,
   Only I call on my divine Idea.

40.

My heart the anvil where my thoughts do beat,
My words the hammers, fashioning my desire,
My breast the forge, including all the heat,
Love is the fuel which maintains the fire;
My sighs the bellows, which the flame increaseth,
Filling mine ears with noise and nightly groaning,
Toiling with pain, my labour never ceaseth,
In grievous passions my woes still bemoaning:
My eyes with tears against the fire striving,
Whose scorching gleed my heart to cinders turneth;
But with those drops the flame again reviving,
Still more and more it to my torment burneth:
   With Sisyphus thus do I roll the stone,
   And turn the wheel with damnèd Ixion.

41.
LOVE'S LUNACY.

Why do I speak of joy, or write of love,
When my heart is the very den of horror,
And in my soul the pains of Hell I prove,
With all his torments and infernal terror?
What should I say? what yet remains to do?
My brain is dry with weeping all too long,
My sighs be spent in uttering of my woe,
And I want words wherewith to tell my wrong:
But still distracted in love's lunacy,
And bedlam-like thus raving in my grief,
Now rail upon her hair, then on her eye;
Now call her goddess, then I call her thief:
   Now I deny her, then I do confess her,
   Now do I curse her, then again I bless her.

42.

SOME men there be who like my method well,
And much commend the strangeness of my vein:
Some say I have a passing pleasing strain,
Some say that in my humour I excel;
Some, who not kindly relish my conceit,
They say, as poets do, I use to feign,
And in bare words paint out my passion's pain;
Thus sundry men their sundry minds repeat:
I pass not, I, how men affected be,
Nor who commends or discommends my verse;
It pleaseth me, if I my woes rehearse,
And in my lines, if she my love may see:
   Only my comfort still consists in this,
   Writing her praise, I cannot write amiss.

43.

WHY should your fair eyes with such sovereign grace
Disperse their rays on every vulgar spirit,
Whilst I in darkness in the self-same place,
Get not one glance to recompense my merit?
So doth the ploughman gaze the wandering star,
And only rest contented with the light,
That never learned what constellations are,
Beyond the bent of his unknowing sight.
O, why should beauty, custom to obey,
To their gross sense apply herself so ill!
Would God I were as ignorant as they,
When I am made unhappy by my skill;
   Only compelled on this poor good to boast,
   Heavens are not kind to them that know them most.

44.

WHILST thus my pen strives to eternize thee,
Age rules my lines with wrinkles in my face,
Where, in the map of all my misery,
Is modelled out the world of my disgrace;
Whilst in despite of tyrannizing times,
Medea-like, I make thee young again,
Proudly thou scorn'st my world-out-wearing rhymes,
And murderest virtue with thy coy disdain:
And though in youth my youth untimely perish,
To keep thee from oblivion and the grave
Ensuing ages yet my rhymes shall cherish,
Where I entombed my better part shall save;
  And though this earthly body fade and die,
  My name shall mount upon eternity.

45.

MUSES which sadly sit about my chair,
Drowned in the tears extorted by my lines,
With heavy sighs whilst thus I break the air,
Painting my passions in these sad designs,
Since she disdains to bless my happy verse,
The strong-built trophies to her living fame,
Ever henceforth my bosom be your hearse,
Wherein the world shall now entomb her name;
Inclose my music, you poor senseless walls,
Since she is deaf, and will not hear my moans,
Soften yourselves with every tear that falls,
Whilst I like Orpheus sing to trees and stones;
  Which with my plaint seem yet with pity moved,
  Kinder than she whom I so long have loved.

46.

PLAIN-PATHED Experience, the unlearnéd's guide,
Her simple followers evidently shows
Sometimes what schoolmen scarcely can decide,
Nor yet wise reason absolutely knows:
In making trial of a murder wrought,
If the vile actors of the heinous deed
Near the dead body haply be brought,
Oft hath been proved the breathless corse will bleed:
She coming near, that my poor heart hath slain,
Long since departed, to the world no more,
The ancient wounds no longer can contain,
But fall to bleeding, as they did before:
   But what of this? Should she to death be led,
   It furthers justice, but helps not the dead.

47.

IN pride of wit, when high desire of fame
Gave life and courage to my labouring pen,
And first the sound and virtue of my name
Won grace and credit in the ears of men;
With those the throngéd theatres that press,
I in the circuit for the laurel strove:
Where the full praise, I freely must confess,
In heat of blood a modest mind might move,
With shouts and claps at every little pause
When the proud round on every side hath rung,
Sadly I sit unmoved with the applause,
As though to me it nothing did belong:
   No public glory vainly I pursue,
   All that I seek is to eternize you.

48.

CUPID, I hate thee, which I'd have thee know;
A naked starveling ever mayst thou be,
Poor rogue, go pawn thy fascia and thy bow,
For some few rags wherewith to cover thee;
Or if thou'lt not thy archery forbear,
To some base rustic do thyself prefer,
And when corn's sown, or grown into the ear,
Practise thy quiver, and turn crow-keeper;
Or being blind, as fittest for the trade,
Go hire thyself some bungling harper's boy;
They that are blind are minstrels often made,
So mayst thou live to thy fair mother's joy:
   That whilst with Mars she holdeth her old way,
   Thou, her blind son, mayst sit by them and play.

49.

THOU leaden brain, which censurest what I write,
And sayst my lines be dull and do not move;
I marvel not thou feel'st not my delight,
Which never feel'st my fiery touch of love,
But thou, whose pen hath like a pack-horse served,
Whose stomach unto gall hath turned thy food,
Whose senses, like poor prisoners, hunger-starved,
Whose grief hath parched thy body, dried thy blood;
Thou which hast scornéd life and hated death,
And in a moment mad, sober, glad, and sorry;
Thou which hast banned thy thoughts, and cursed thy birth
With thousand plagues more than in Purgatory:
   Thou, thus whose spirit love in his fire refines,
   Come thou and read, admire, applaud my lines.

50.

As in some countries far remote from hence,
The wretched creature destinéd to die,
Having the judgment due to his offence,
By surgeons begged, their art on him to try,
Which on the living work without remorse,
First make incision on each mastering vein,
Then stanch the bleeding, then transpierce the corse,
And with their balms recure the wounds again,
Then poison and with physic him restore :
Not that they fear the hopeless man to kill,
But their experience to increase the more :
Even so my mistress works upon my ill ;
 By curing me and killing me each hour,
 Only to show her beauty's sovereign power.

51.

Calling to mind since first my love begun,
The uncertain times oft varying in their course,
How things still unexpectedly have run,
As't please the Fates by their resistless force :
Lastly, mine eyes amazedly have seen
Essex' great fall, Tyrone his peace to gain,
The quiet end of that long-living Queen,
This King's fair entrance, and our peace with Spain,
We and the Dutch at length ourselves to sever ;
Thus the world doth and evermore shall reel ;
Yet to my goddess am I constant ever,
Howe'er blind Fortune turn her giddy wheel :
 Though heaven and earth prove both to me untrue
 Yet am I still inviolate to you.

52.

WHAT, dost thou mean to cheat me of my heart,
To take all mine and give me none again?
Or have thine eyes such magic, or that art
That what they get they ever do retain?
Play not the tyrant, but take some remorse,
Rebate thy spleen if but for pity's sake;
Or cruel, if·thou canst not, let us scorse,
And for one piece of thine my whole heart take.
But what of pity do I speak to thee,
Whose breast is proof against complaint or prayer?
Or can I think what my reward shall be
From that proud beauty which was my betrayer;
   What talk I of a heart when thou hast none?
   Or if thou hast, it is a flinty one,

53.
ANOTHER TO THE RIVER ANKOR.

CLEAR Ankor, on whose silver-sanded shore
My soul-shrined saint, my fair Idea, lies;
O blessèd brook, whose milk-white swans adore
The crystal stream refinèd by her eyes,
Where sweet myrrh-breathing zephyr in the spring
Gently distils his nectar-dropping showers,
Where nightingales in Arden sit and sing
Amongst the dainty dew-impearlèd flowers;
Say thus, fair brook, when thou shalt see thy queen,
Lo, here thy shepherd spent his wandering years,
And in these shades, dear nymph, he oft hath been,
And here to thee he sacrificed his tears:
   Fair Arden, thou my Tempe art alone,
   And thou, sweet Ankor, art my Helicon.

54.

YET read at last the story of my woe,
The dreary abstracts of my endless cares,
With my life's sorrow interlinéd so,
Smoked with my sighs and blotted with my tears,
The sad memorials of my miseries
Penned in the grief of mine afflicted ghost,
My life's complaint in doleful elegies,
With so pure love as time could never boast;
Receive the incense which I offer here,
By my strong faith ascending to thy fame:
My zeal, my hope, my vows, my praise, my prayer,
My soul's oblations to thy sacred name;
    Which name my Muse to highest heavens shall raise,
    By chaste desire, true love, and virtuous praise.

55.

MY fair, if thou wilt register my love,
A world of volumes shall thereof arise;
Preserve my tears, and thou thyself shalt prove
A second flood down raining from mine eyes:
Note but my sighs, and thine eyes shall behold
The sunbeams smothered with immortal smoke;
And if by thee my prayers may be enrolled,
They heaven and earth to pity shall provoke:
Look thou into my breast, and thou shalt see
Chaste holy vows for my soul's sacrifice;
That soul, sweet maid, which so hath honoured thee
Erecting trophies to thy sacred eyes,
    Those eyes to my heart shining ever bright
    When darkness hath obscured each other light.

56.

AN ALLUSION TO THE EAGLETS.

WHEN like an eaglet I first found my love,
For that the virtue I thereof would know,
Upon the nest I set it forth to prove
If it were of that kingly kind or no:
But it no sooner saw my sun appear,
But on her rays with open eyes it stood,
To show that I had hatched it for the air,
And rightly came from that brave mounting brood;
And when the plumes were summed with sweet desire,
To prove the pinions it ascends the skies:
Do what I could, it need'ly would aspire
To my soul's sun those two celestial eyes:
   Thus from my breast, where it was bred alone,
   It after thee is like an eaglet flown.

57.

YOU, best discerned of my mind's inward eyes,
And yet your graces outwardly divine,
Whose dear remembrance in my bosom lies,
Too rich a relic for so poor a shrine:
You, in whom Nature chose herself to view,
When she her own perfection would admire,
Bestowing all her excellence on you;
At whose pure eyes Love lights his hallowed fire,—
Even as a man that in some trance hath seen
More than his wondering utterance can unfold,
That rapt in spirit in better worlds hath been,
So must your praise distractedly be told;
   Most of all short when I should show you most
   In your perfections so much am I lost.

58.

IN former times, such as had store of coin,
In wars at home, or when for conquests bound,
For fear that some their treasure should purloin,
Gave it to keep to spirits within the ground;
And to attend it them as strongly tied
Till they returned home; when they never came,
Such as by art to get the same have tried
From the strong spirit, by no means force the same,
Nearer men come that further flies away,
Striving to hold it strongly in the deep:
Even as this spirit, so you alone do play
With those rich beauties Heaven gives you to keep;
  Pity so left to the coldness of your blood,
  Not to avail you nor do others good.

59.
TO PROVERB.

As Love and I late harboured in one inn,
With proverbs thus each other entertain:
" In love there is no lack," thus I begin;
" Fair words make fools," replieth he again:
" Who spares to speak doth spare to speed," quoth I;
" As well," saith he, " too forward as too slow:"
" Fortune assists the boldest," I reply;
" A hasty man," quoth he, " ne'er wanted woe:"
" Labour is light where love," quoth I, " doth pay;"
Saith he, " Light burthen's heavy, if far borne:"
Quoth I, " The main lost, cast the bye away;"
" You have spun a fair thread," he replies in scorn.
  And having thus a while each other thwarted,
  Fools as we met, so fools again we parted.

60.

DEFINE my weal and tell the joys of Heaven,
Express my woes and show the pains of Hell,
Declare what fate unlucky stars have given,
And ask a world upon my life to dwell;
Make known the faith that Fortune could not move,
Compare my worth with others' base desert,
Let virtue be the touchstone of my love,
So may the heavens read wonders in my heart;
Behold the clouds which have eclipsed my sun,
And view the crosses which my course do let,
Tell me if ever since the world begun
So fair a rising had so foul a set:
    And see if Time, if he would strive to prove,
    Can show a second to so pure a love.

61.

SINCE there's no help, come let us kiss and part,
Nay, I have done, you get no more of me,
And I am glad, yea, glad with all my heart,
That thus so cleanly I myself can free;
Shake hands for ever, cancel all our vows,
And when we meet at any time again,
Be it not seen in either of our brows
That we one jot of former love retain;
Now at the last gasp of Love's latest breath,
When, his pulse failing, passion speechless lies,
When Faith is kneeling by his bed of death,
And Innocence is closing up his eyes,
    Now if thou wouldst, when all have given him over,
    From death to life thou might'st him yet recover.

62.

WHEN first I ended, then I first began,
Then more I travelled, further from my rest,
Where most I lost there most of all I won,
Pinéd with hunger rising from a feast.
Methinks I fly, yet want I legs to go,
Wise in conceit, in act a very sot,
Ravished with joy amidst a hell of woe,
What most I seem that surest am I not.
I build my hopes a world above the sky,
Yet with the mole I creep into the earth;
In plenty I am starved with penury,
And yet I surfeit in the greatest dearth:
    I have, I want, despair, and yet desire,
      Burned in a sea of ice, drowned 'midst a fire.

63.

TRUCE, gentle love, a parley now I crave,
Methinks 'tis long since first these wars begun,
Nor thou, nor I, the better yet can have,
Bad is the match where neither party won.
I offer free conditions of fair peace,
My heart for hostage that it shall remain,
Discharge our forces, here let malice cease,
So for my pledge thou give me pledge again;
Or if nothing but death will serve thy turn,
Still thirsting for subversion of my state,
Do what thou canst, raze, massacre, and burn,
Let the world see the utmost of thy hate;
    I send defiance, since, if overthrown,
      Thou vanquishing, the conquest is mine own.

ELEGIES

UPON SUNDRY OCCASIONS.

OF HIS LADY'S NOT COMING TO LONDON.

THAT ten-years-travelled Greek returned from sea
Ne'er joyed so much to see his Ithaca
As I should you, who are alone to me
More than wide Greece could to that wanderer be.
The winter winds still easterly do keep,
And with keen frosts have chainéd up the deep ;
The sun's to us a niggard of his rays,
But revelleth with our Antipodes ;
And seldom to us when he shows his head,
Muffled in vapours he straight hies to bed.
In those bleak mountains can you live, where snow
Maketh the vales up to the hills to grow ;
Whereas men's breaths do instantly congeal
And atomed mists turn instantly to hail ;
Belike you think, from this more temperate coast
My sighs may have the power to thaw the frost,
Which I from hence should swiftly send you thither,
Yet not so swift as you come slowly hither.
How many a time hath Phœbe from her wane
With Phœbus' fires filled up her horns again ;

She through her orb still on her course doth range,
But you keep yours still, nor for me will change ;
The sun that mounted the stern Lion's back,
Shall with the Fishes shortly dive the brack,
But still you keep your station which confines
You, nor regard him travelling the signs.
Those ships which when you went put out to sea,
Both to our Greenland and Virginia,
Are now returned, and customed have their fraught,
Yet you arrive not, nor return me aught.
    The Thames was not so frozen yet this year
As is my bosom, with the chilly fear
Of your not coming, which on me doth light
As on those climes where half the world is night.
    Of every tedious hour you have made two
All this long winter here, by missing you : ·
Minutes are months, and when the hour is past
A year is ended since the clock struck last,
When your remembrance puts me on the rack,
And I should swoon to see an Almanack,
To read what silent weeks away are slid
Since the dire Fates you from my sight have hid.
    I hate him who the first deviser was
Of this same foolish thing, the hour-glass,
And of the watch whose dribbling sands and wheel,
With their slow strokes, make me too much to feel
Your slackness hither. O how I do ban
Him that these dials against walls began,
Whose snaily motion of the moving hand,
Although it go, yet seem to me to stand ;
As though at Adam it had first set out,
And had been stealing all this while about,
And when it back to the first point should come,
It shall be then just at the general doom.

The seas into themselves retract their flows,
The changing wind from every quarter blows,
Declining winter in the spring doth call,
The stars rise to us as from us they fall;
Those birds we see that leave us in the prime
Again in autumn re-salute our clime.
Sure, either Nature you from kind hath made,
Or you delight else to be retrograde.
   But I perceive, by your attractive powers,
Like an enchantress you have charmed the hours
Into short minutes, and have drawn them back,
So that of us at London you do lack
Almost a year; the spring is scarce begun
There where you live, and autumn almost done
With us more eastward; surely you devise,
By your strong magic, that the sun shall rise
Where now it sets, and that in some few years
You'll alter quite the motion of the spheres.
   Yes, and you mean I shall complain my love
To gravelled walks or to a stupid grove,
Now your companions; and that you the while,
As you are cruel, will sit by and smile,
To make me write to these, while passers-by
Slightly look in your lovely face where I
See beauty's heaven, whilst silly blockheads they,
Like laden asses, plod upon their way
And wonder not, as you should point a clown
Up to the Guards, or Ariadne's crown
Of constellations, and his dulness tell,
He'd think your words were certainly a spell;
Or him some piece from Crete or Marcus show,
In all his life which till that time ne'er saw
Painting except, in alehouse or old Hall
Done by some druzzler, of the Prodigal.

Nay do, stay still, whilst time away shall steal
Your youth and beauty, and yourself conceal
From me, I pray you ; you have now inured
Me to your absence, and I have endured
Your want this long, whilst I have starvéd been
For your short letters, as you held it sin
To write to me, that to appease my woe,
I read o'er those you writ a year ago,
Which are to me as though they had been made
Long time before the first Olympiad.
    For thanks and courtesies sell your presence then
To tattling women and to things like men,
And be more foolish than the Indians are,
For bells, for knives, for glasses, and such ware,
That sell their pearl and gold ; but here I stay,
So would I not have you but come away.

TO

MASTER GEORGE SANDYS,

Treasurer for the English Colony in Virginia.

FRIEND, if you think my papers may supply
You with some strange omitted novelty
Which others' letters yet have left untold,
You take me off before I can take hold
Of you at all : I put not thus to sea
For two months' voyage to Virginia,
With news which now's a little something here,
But will be nothing ere it can come there.

I fear as I do stabbing this word, State,
I dare not speak of the Palatinate,
Although some men make it their hourly theme,
And talk what's done in Austria and in Beam,
I may not so ; what Spinola intends,
Nor with his Dutch which way Prince Maurice bends;
To other men although these things be free,
Yet, George, they must be mysteries to me.
    I scarce dare praise a virtuous friend that's dead,
Lest for my lines he should be censuréd ;
It was my hap before all other men
To suffer shipwreck by my forward pen
When King James entered, at which joyful time
I taught his title to this isle in rhyme,
And to my part did all the Muses win,
With high-pitch pæans to applaud him in :
When cowardice had tied up every tongue,
And all stood silent, yet for him I sung ;
And when before by danger I was dared,
I kicked her from me, nor a jot I spared.
Yet had not my clear spirit in Fortune's scorn,
Me above earth and her afflictions borne,
He next my God on whom I built my trust
Had left me trodden lower than the dust :
But let this pass ; in the extremest ill,
Apollo's brood must be courageous still,
Let pies and daws sit dumb before their death,
Only the swan sings at the parting breath.
    And, worthy George, by industry and use,
Let's see what lines Virginia will produce;
Go on with Ovid, as you have begun
With the first five books ; let your numbers run
Glib as the former, so shall it live long,
And do much honour to the English tongue ;

Entice the Muses thither to repair,
Entreat them gently, train them to that air,
For they from hence may thither hap to fly,
T'wards the sad time which but too fast doth hie ;
For poesie is followed with such spite
By grovelling drones that never wrought her height,
That she must hence, she may no longer stay ;
The dreary Fates prefixéd have the day
Of her departure, which is now come on,
And they command her straightways to be gone ;
That bestial herd so hotly her pursue,
And to her succour there be very few,
Nay, none at all, her wrongs that will redress,
But she must wander in the wilderness,
Like to the woman which that holy John
Beheld in Patmos in his vision.
    As the English now, so did the stiffnecked Jews
Their noble Prophets utterly refuse,
And of those men such poor opinions had,
They counted Isaiah and Ezekiel mad ;
When Jeremy his Lamentations writ,
They thought the wizard quite out of his wit,
Such sots they were as worthily to lie
Locked in the chains of their captivity.
Knowledge hath still her eddy in her flow,
So it hath been, and it will still be so.
    That famous Greece where learning flourished most,
Hath of her Muses long since left to boast,
The unlettered Turk and rude barbarian trades
Where Homer sang his lofty Iliads ;
And this vast volume of the world hath taught
Much may to pass in little time be brought.
    As if to symptoms we may credit give,
This very time wherein we two now live

Shall in the compass wound the Muses more
Than all the old English ignorance before,
Base ballatry is so beloved and sought,
And those brave numbers are put by for nought,
Which rarely read, were able to awake
Bodies from graves, and to the ground to shake
The wandering clouds, and to our men-at-arms
'Gainst pikes and muskets were most powerful charms.
That but I know ensuing ages shall
Raise her again who now is in her fall,
And out of dust reduce our scattered rhymes,
The rejected jewels of these slothful times,
Who with the Muses would misspend an hour,
But let blind Gothish barbarism devour
These feverous dog-days, blest by no recórd,
But to be everlastingly abhorred.
    If you vouchsafe rescription, stuff your quill
With natural bounties, and impart your skill
In the description of the place, that I
May become learnéd in the soil thereby;
Of noble Wyat's health, and let me hear
The Governor; and how our people there
Increase and labour, what supplies are sent,
Which I confess shall give me much content;
But you may save your labour, if you please,
To write to me aught of your savages.
As savage slaves be in Great Britain here
As any one that you can show me there,
And though for this I'll say I do not thirst,
Yet I should like it well to be the first
Whose numbers hence into Virginia flew,
So, noble Sandys, for this time adieu.

TO
MASTER WILLIAM JEFFREYS,
Chaplain to the Lord Ambassador in Spain.

MY noble friend, you challenge me to write
To you in verse, and often you recite
My promise to you, and to send you news.
As 'tis a thing I very seldom use,
And I must write of State, if to Madrid,
A thing our proclamations here forbid,
And that word State such latitude doth bear,
As it may make me very well to fear
To write, nay, speak at all, these let you know
Your power on me; yet not that I will show
The love I bear you in that lofty height,
So clear expression, or such words of weight,
As into Spanish if they were translated,
Might make the poets of that realm amated.
Yet these my least were, but that you extort
These numbers from me, when I should report
In homespun prose, in good plain honest words,
The news our woful England us affords.
    The Muses here sit sad, and muse the while
A sort of swine unseasonably defile
Those sacred springs, which from the bi-cliff hill
Dropt their pure nectar into every quill;
In this with State I hope I do not deal,
This only tends the Muses' commonweal.
    What canst thou hope or look for from his pen
Who lives with beasts, though in the shapes of men?
And what a poor few are we honest still,
And dare to be so when all the world is ill.

I find this age of ours marked with this fate,
That honest men are still precipitate
Under base villains, which till the earth can vent
This her last brood, and wholly hath them spent,
Shall be so; then in resolution shall
Virtue again arise by vice's fall.
But that shall I not see, neither will I
Maintain this, as one doth a prophecy,
That our King James to Rome shall surely go,
And from his chair the Pope shall overthrow.
But O, this world is so given up to hell,
That as the old giants, which did once rebel
Against the gods, so this now living race
Dare sin, yet stand, and jeer Heaven in the face.
 But soft, my Muse, and make a little stay,
Surely thou art not rightly in thy way.
To my good Jeffreys was not I about
To write, and see, I suddenly am out;
This is pure satire that thou speak'st, and I
Was first in hand to write an elegy.
To tell my country's shame I not delight,
But do bemoan it I am no Democrite.
O God, though virtue mightily do grieve,
For all this world yet will I not believe
But that she's fair and lovely, and that she
So to the period of the world shall be;
Else had she been forsaken sure of all,
For that so many sundry mischiefs fall
Upon her daily, and so many take
Arms up against her, as it well might make
Her to forsake her nature, and behind
To leave no step for future time to find,
As she had never been: for he that now
Can do her most disgrace, him they allow

The time's chief champion, and he is the man
The prize and palm that absolutely won.
For where King's closets her free seat hath been,
She, near the lodge, not suffered is to inn,
For ignorance against her stands in state,
Like some great porter at a palace gate.
So dull and barbarous lately are we grown,
And there are some this slavery that have sown,
That for man's knowledge it enough doth make
If he can learn to read an Almanack,
By whom that trash of Amadis de Gaul
Is held an author most authentical;
And things we have like noblemen that be
In little time, which I have hope to see
Upon their foot-cloths, as the streets they ride,
To have their horn-books at their girdles tied;
But all their superfluity of spite
On virtue's handmaid Poesy doth light,
And to extirp her all their plots they lay,
But to her ruin they shall miss the way;
For 'tis alone the monuments of wit
Above the rage of tyrants that do sit,
And from their strength not one himself can save,
But they shall triumph o'er his hated grave.

 In my conceit, friend, thou didst never see
A righter madman than thou hast of me,
For now as elegiac I bewail
These poor base times, then suddenly I rail
And am satiric; not that I enforce
Myself to be so, but even as remorse
Or hate, in the proud fulness of their height
Master my fancy, just so do I write.

 But, gentle friend, as soon shall I behold
That stone of which so many have us told,

(Yet never any to this day could make)
The great Elixir, or to undertake
The Rose-Cross knowledge, which is much like that,
A tarrying-iron for fools to labour at,
As ever after I may hope to see
(A plague upon this beastly world for me)
Wit so respected as it was of yore.
And if hereafter any it restore,
It must be those that yet for many a year
Shall be unborn, that must inhabit here;
And such in virtue as shall be ashamed
Almost to hear their ignorant grandsires named,
With whom so many noble spirits then lived,
That were by them of all reward deprived.

    My noble friend, I would I might have quit
This age of these, and that I might have writ,
Before all other, how much the brave pen
Had here been honoured of the Englishmen;
Goodness and knowledge held by them in prize;
How hateful to them ignorance and vice;
But it falls out the contrary is true,
And so, my Jeffreys, for this time adieu.

TO MY MOST DEARLY LOVED FRIEND,

HENRY REYNOLDS, Esquire.

Of Poets and Poesie.

MY dearly lovéd friend, how oft have we
In winter evenings, meaning to be free,
To some well-chosen place used to retire,
And there, with moderate meat and wine and fire,
Have passed the hours contentedly with chat,
Now talked of this, and then discoursed of that,
Spoke our own verses 'twixt ourselves ; if not,
Other men's lines, which we by chance had got,
Or some stage pieces famous long before,
Of which your happy memory had store ;
And I remember you much pleaséd were
Of those who livéd long ago to hear,
As well as of those of these latter times
Who have enriched our language with their rhymes,
And in succession how still up they grew,
Which is the subject that I now pursue :
For from my cradle, you must know that I
Was still inclined to noble poesy,
And when that once Pueriles I had read,
And newly had my Cato construéd,
In my small self I greatly marvelled then,
Amongst all other, what strange kind of men
These poets were ; and, pleaséd with the name,
To my mild tutor merrily I came,
(For I was then a proper goodly page,
Much like a pigmy, scarce ten years of age)

Clasping my slender arms about his thigh.
" O, my dear master! cannot you," quoth I,
Make me a poet? Do it if you can,
And you shall see I'll quickly be a man."
Who me thus answered, smiling, " Boy," quoth he,
" If you'll not play the wag, but I may see
You ply your learning, I will shortly read
Some poets to you." Phœbus be my speed,
To 't hard went I, when shortly he began,
And first read to me honest Mantuan,
Then Virgil's Eclogues; being entered thus,
Methought I straight had mounted Pegasus,
And in his full career could make him stop
And bound upon Parnassus bi-cliff top.
I scorned your ballad then, though it were done
And had for finis William Elderton.
But soft, in sporting with this childish jest,
I from my subject have too long digrest,
Then to the matter that we took in hand,
Jove and Apollo for the Muses stand.

That noble Chaucer in those former times,
The first enriched our English with his rhymes,
And was the first of ours that ever brake
Into the Muses' treasure, and first spake
In weighty numbers, delving in the mine
Of perfect knowledge, which he could refine
And coin for current, and as much as then
The English language could express to men
He made it do, and by his wondrous skill
Gave us much light from his abundant quill.

And honest Gower, who in respect of him
Had only sipped at Aganippas' brim,
And though in years this last was him before,
Yet fell he far short of the other's store.

When after those, four ages very near,
They with the Muses which conversèd were
That princely Surrey, early in the time
Of the Eighth Henry, who was then the prime
Of England's noble youth ; with him there came
Wyat, with reverence whom we still do name ;
Amongst our poets Brian had a share
With the two former, which accounted are
That time's best makers and the authors were
Of those small poems which the title bear
Of songs and sonnets, wherein oft they hit
On many dainty passages of wit.

Gascoigne and Churchyard after them again,
In the beginning of Eliza's reign,
Accounted were great meterers many a day,
But not inspirèd with brave fire ; had they
Lived but a little longer, they had seen
Their works before them to have buried been.

Grave, moral Spenser after these came on,
Than whom I am persuaded there was none,
Since the blind bard his Iliads up did make,
Fitter a task like that to undertake ;
To set down boldly, bravely to invent,
In all high knowledge surely excellent.

The noble Sidney with this last arose,
That hero was for numbers and for prose,
That throughly paced our language, as to show
The plenteous English hand in hand might go
With Greek and Latin, and did first reduce
Our tongue from Lyly's writing then in use ;
Talking of stones, stars, plants, of fishes, flies,
Playing with words and idle similes ;
As the English, apes and very zanies be
Of everything that they do hear and see,

So imitating his ridiculous tricks,
They spake and writ all like mere lunatics.
  Then Warner, though his lines were not so trimmed,
Nor yet his poem so exactly limned
And neatly jointed but the critic may
Easily reprove him, yet thus let me say
For my old friend, some passages there be
In him which I protest have taken me
With almost wonder, so fine, clear and new,
As yet they have been equalléd by few.
  Neat Marlowe, bathéd in the Thespian springs,
Had in him those brave translunary things
That the first poets had, his raptures were
All air and fire, which made his verses clear;
For that fine madness still he did retain
Which rightly should possess a poet's brain.
  And surely Nash, though he a proser were,
A branch of laurel yet deserves to bear,
Sharply satiric was he, and that way
He went, since that his being to this day
Few have attempted, and I surely think
Those words shall hardly be set down with ink
Shall scorch and blast so as his could, where he
Would inflict vengeance; and be it said of thee,
Shakespeare, thou hadst as smooth a comic vein,
Fitting the sock, and in thy natural brain
As strong conception and as clear a rage,
As any one that trafficked with the stage.
  Amongst these Samuel Daniel, whom if I
May speak of, but to censure do deny,
Only have heard some wise men him rehearse
To be too much historian in verse;
His rhymes were smooth, his metres well did close,
But yet his manner better fitted prose.

Next these, learned Jonson in this list I bring,
Who had drunk deep of the Pierian spring,
Whose knowledge did him worthily prefer,
And long was lord here of the theatre,
Who in opinion made our learnedst to stick
Whether in poems rightly dramatic,
Strong Seneca or Plautus, he or they
Should bear the buskin or the sock away.
Others again here livéd in my days,
That have of us deservéd no less praise
For their translations, than the daintiest wit
That on Parnassus thinks he high'st doth sit,
And for a chair may 'mongst the Muses call,
As the most curious maker of them all;
As reverend Chapman, who hath brought to us
Musæus, Homer, and Hesiodus
Out of the Greek; and by his skill hath reared
Them to that height, and to our tongue endeared,
That were those poets at this day alive,
To see their books thus with us to survive,
They would think, having neglected them so long,
They had been written in the English tongue.

And Silvester who from the French more weak
Made Bartas of his six days' labour speak
In natural English, who, had he there stayed
He had done well, and never had bewrayed
His own invention to have been so poor,
Who still wrote less in striving to write more.

Then dainty Sandys, that hath to English done
Smooth sliding Ovid, and hath made him run
With so much sweetness and unusual grace,
As though the neatness of the English pace
Should tell the letting Latin that it came
But slowly after, as though stiff and lame.

So Scotland sent us hither for our own
That man, whose name I ever would have known
To stand by mine, that most ingenious knight,
My Alexander, to whom in his right
I want extremely, yet in speaking thus
I do but show the love that was 'twixt us,
And not his numbers, which were brave and high,
So like his mind was his clear poesie;
And my dear Drummond, to whom much I owe
For his much love, and proud I was to know
His poesie, for which two worthy men,
I Menstry still shall love, and Hawthornden.
Then the two Beaumonts and my Browne arose,
My dear companions, whom I freely chose
My bosom friends; and in their several ways
Rightly born poets, and in these last days
Men of much note, and no less nobler parts,
Such as have freely told to me their hearts,
As I have mine to them. But if you shall
Say in your knowledge that these be not all
Have writ in numbers, be informed that I
Only myself to these few men do tie,
Whose works oft printed, set on every post,
To public censure subject have been most.
For such whose poems, be they ne'er so rare,
In private chambers that encloistered are,
And by transcription daintily must go
As though the world unworthy were to know
Their rich composures, let those men that keep
These wondrous relics in their judgment deep,
And cry them up so, let such pieces be
Spoke of by those that shall come after me,
I pass not for them; nor do mean to run
In quest of these that them applause have won,

Upon our stages in these latter days,
That are so many, let them have their bays
That do deserve it ; let those wits that haunt
Those public circuits, let them freely chaunt
Their fine composures and their praise pursue,
And so, my dear friend, for this time adieu.

The Quest of Cynthia.

WHAT time the groves were clad in green,
   The fields drest all in flowers,
And that the sleek-haired nymphs were seen
   To seek them summer bowers;

Forth roved I by the sliding rills
   To find where Cynthia sat,
Whose name so often from the hills
   The echoes wondered at.

When me upon my quest to bring,
   That pleasure might excel,
The birds strove which should sweetliest sing,
   The flowers which sweet'st should smell.

"Long wandering in the woods," said I,
   "Oh, whither's Cynthia gone?"
When soon the echo doth reply
   To my last word, "Go on."

At length upon a lofty fir
   It was my chance to find,
Where that dear name most due to her
   Was carved upon the rind.

Which whilst with wonder I beheld,
  The bees their honey brought,
And up the carvéd letters filled,
  As they with gold were wrought.

And near that tree's more spacious root,
  Then looking on the ground,
The shape of her most dainty foot
  Imprinted there I found ;

Which stuck there like a curious seal,
  As though it should forbid
Us, wretched mortals, to reveal
  What under it was hid.

Besides the flowers which it had prest
  Appearéd to my view,
More fresh and lovely than the rest
  That in the meadows grew ·

The clear drops in the steps that stood
  Of that delicious girl,
The nymphs amongst their dainty food
  Drunk for dissolvéd pearl.

The yielding sand where she had trod,
  Untouched yet with the wind,
By the fair posture plainly showed
  Where I might Cynthia find.

When on upon my wayless walk,
  As my desires me draw,
I like a madman fell to talk
  With everything I saw ;

I asked some lilies why so white
  They from their fellows were;
Who answered me that Cynthia's sight
  Had made them look so clear.

I asked a nodding violet why
  It sadly hung the head,
It told me Cynthia late passed by,
  Too soon from it she fled.

A bed of roses saw I there,
  Bewitching with their grace;
Besides so wondrous sweet they were
  That they perfumed the place;

I of a shrub of those inquired,
  From others of that kind,
Who with such virtue them inspired,
  It answered (to my mind):

" As the base hemlock were we such,
  The poisoned'st weed that grows,
Till Cynthia by her godlike touch
  Transformed us to the rose:

" Since when those frosts that winter brings
  Which candy every green
Renew us like the teeming springs,
  And we thus fresh are seen."

At length I on a fountain light,
  Whose brim with pinks was platted;
The bank with daffodilies dight,
  With grass like sleave was matted,

THE QUEST OF CYNTHIA.

When I demanded of that well
    What power frequented there,
Desiring it would please to tell
    What name it used to bear :

It told me it was Cynthia's own,
    Within whose cheerful brims
That curious nymph had oft been known
    To bathe her snowy limbs.

Since when that water had the power
    Lost maidenheads to restore,
And make one twenty in an hour,
    Of Eson's age before.

And told me that the bottom clear,
    Now laid with many a set
Of seed-pearl, ere she bathéd her there
    Was known as black as jet ;

As when she from the water came,
    Where first she touched the mould,
In balls the people made the same
    For pomander, and sold.

When chance me to an arbour led,
    Whereas I might behold
Two blest Elyisums in one stead,
    The less the great enfold.

The place which she had chosen out
    Herself in to repose ;
Had they come down, the gods no doubt
    The very same had chose.

The wealthy spring yet never bore
   That sweet nor dainty flower
That damasked not the chequered floor
   Of Cynthia's summer bower.

The birch, the myrtle, and the bay,
   Like friends did all embrace ;
And their large branches did display
   To canopy the place.

Where she like Venus doth appear
   Upon a rosy bed ;
As lilies the soft pillows were
   Whereon she laid her head.

Heaven on her shape such cost bestowed,
   And with such bounties blest,
No limb of hers but might have made
   A goddess at the least.

The flies by chance meshed in her hair,
   By the bright radiance thrown
From her clear eyes rich jewels were,
   They so like diamonds shone.

The meanest weed the soil there bare
   Her breath did so refine,
That it with woodbine durst compare,
   And beard the eglantine.

The dew which on the tender grass
   The evening had distilled,
To pure rose-water turnéd was,
   The shades with sweets that filled.

The winds were hushed, no leaf so small
   At all was seen to stir:
Whilst tuning to the water's fall
   The small birds sang to her.

Where she too quickly me espies,
   When I might plainly see
A thousand Cupids from her eyes
   Shoot all at once at me.

" Into these secret shades," cried she,
   " How dar'st thou be so bold
To enter, consecrate to me,
   Or touch this hallowed mould?

" Those words," she said, " I can pronounce,
   Which to that shape can bring
Thee, which the hunter had who once
   Saw Dian in the spring."

" Bright nymph," again I thus reply,
   " This cannot me affright:
I had rather in thy presence die
   Than live out of thy sight.

" I first upon the mountains high
   Built altars to thy name,
And graved it on the rocks thereby,
   To propagate thy fame.

" I taught the shepherds on the downs
   Of thee to frame their lays:
'Twas I that filled the neighbouring towns
   With ditties of thy praise.

"Thy colours I devised with care,
  Which were unknown before;
Which, since that, in their braided hair
  The nymphs and silvans wore.

"Transform me to what shape you can,
  I pass not what it be:
Yea, what most hateful is to man,
  So I may follow thee."

Which when she heard, full pearly floods
  I in her eyes might view;
Quoth she, "Most welcome to these woods,
  Too mean for one so true.

"Here from the hateful world we'll live,
  A den of mere despite,
To idiots only that doth give,
  Which be her sole delight;

"To people the infernal pit
  That more and more doth strive;
Where only villany is wit,
  And devils only thrive.

"Whose vileness us shall never awe,
  But here our sports shall be
Such as the golden world first saw,
  Most innocent and free.

"Of simples in these groves that grow
  We'll learn the perfect skill,
The nature of each herb to know,
  Which cures, and which can kill.

"The waxen palace of the bee,
  We seeking will surprise,
The curious workmanship to see
  Of her full laden thighs.

"We'll suck the sweets out of the comb,
  And make the gods repine
As they do feast in Jove's great room,
  To see with what we dine.

"Yet when there haps a honey fall,
  We'll lick the syruped leaves;
And tell the bees that theirs is gall
  To this upon the greaves.

"The nimble squirrel noting here,
  Her mossy dray that makes,
And laugh to see the lusty deer
  Come bounding o'er the brakes.

"The spider's web to watch we'll stand,
  And when it takes the bee,
We'll help out of the tyrant's hand
  The innocent to free.

"Sometimes we'll angle at the brook,
  The freckled trout to take
With silken worms, and bait the hook
  Which him our prey shall make.

"Of meddling with such subtle tools,
  Such dangers that enclose,
The moral is that painted fools
  Are caught with silken shows.

"And when the moon doth once appear
  We'll trace the lower grounds,
When Fairies in their ringlets there
  Do dance their nightly rounds.

"And have a flock of turtle-doves
  A guard on us to keep;
As witness of our honest loves,
  To watch us till we sleep."

Which spoke, I felt such holy fires
  To overspread my breast,
As lent life to my chaste desires
  And gave me endless rest.

By Cynthia thus do I subsist,
  On earth Heaven's only pride:
Let her be mine, and let who list
  Take all the world beside.

The Shepherd's Sirena.

DORILUS in sorrows deep,
Autumn waxing old and chill,
As he sate his flocks to keep,
Underneath an easy hill :
Chanced to cast his eye aside
On those fields where he had seen
Bright Sirena, Nature's pride,
Sporting on the pleasant green :
To whose walks the shepherds oft
Came her godlike foot to find,
And in places that were soft
Kissed the print there left behind ;
Where the path which she had trod
Hath thereby more glory gained
Than in heaven that milky road
Which with nectar Hebe stained ;
But bleak winter's boist'rous blasts
Now their fading pleasures chid,
And so filled them with his wastes,
That from sight her steps were hid.
Silly shepherd, sad the while,
For his sweet Sirena gone,
All his pleasures in exile,
Laid on the cold earth alone.

Whilst his gamesome cut-tailed cur
With his mirthless master plays,
Striving him with sport to stir
As in his more youthful days,
Dorilus his dog doth chide,
Lays his well-tuned bagpipe by,
And his sheep-hook casts aside:
"There," quoth he, "together lie."
When a letter forth he took
Which to him Sirena writ,
With a deadly downcast look,
And thus fell to reading it.
  "Dorilus, my dear," quoth she,
"Kind companion of my woe,
Though we thus divided be,
Death cannot divorce us so:
Thou whose bosom hath been still
The only closet of my care,
And in all my good and ill
Ever had thy equal share;
Might I win thee from thy fold,
Thou shouldst come to visit me,
But the winter is so cold
That I fear to hazard thee:
The wild waters are waxed high,
So they are both deaf and dumb,
Loved they thee so well as I,
They would ebb when thou shouldst come;
Then my cot with light should shine
Purer than the vestal fire;
Nothing here but should be thine
That thy heart can well desire;
Where at large we will relate
From what cause our friendship grew,

And in that the varying fate
Since we first each other knew :
Of my heavy passéd plight,
As of many a future fear,
Which, except the silent night,
None but only thou shalt hear.
My sad heart it shall relieve
When my thoughts I shall disclose,
For thou canst not choose but grieve
When I shall recount my woes ;
There is nothing to that friend
To whose close uncrannied breast
We our secret thought may send
And there safely let it rest ;
And thy faithful counsel may
My distresséd case assist,
Sad affliction else may sway
Me, a woman, as it list.
Hither I would have thee haste,
Yet would gladly have thee stay,
When those dangers I forecast
That may meet thee by the way.
Do as thou shalt think it best,
Let thy knowledge be thy guide,
Live thou in my constant breast,
Whatsoever shall betide."

He her letter having read,
Puts it in his scrip again,
Looking like a man half dead,
By her kindness strangely slain ;
And as one who only knew
Her distresséd present state,
And to her had still been true,
Thus doth with himself dilate :

"I will not thy face admire,
Admirable though it be,
Nor thine eyes whose subtle fire
So much wonder win in me:
But my marvel shall be now,
And of long it hath been so,
Of all womankind that thou
Wert ordained to taste of woe;
To a beauty so divine,
Paradise in little done,
O that Fortune should assign
Aught but what thou well might'st shun;
But my counsels such must be,
Though as yet I them conceal,
By their deadly wound in me
They thy hurt must only heal;
Could I give what thou dost crave,
To that pass thy state is grown,
I thereby thy life may save,
But am sure to lose mine own;
To that joy thou dost conceive,
Through my heart the way doth lie,
Which in two for thee must cleave
Lest that thou shouldst go awry.
Thus my death must be a toy
Which my pensive breast must cover;
Thy belovéd to enjoy
Must be taught thee by thy lover.
Hard the choice I have to choose,
To myself if friend I be,
I must my Sirena lose,
If not so, she loseth me."
 Thus whilst he doth cast about
What therein were best to do,

Nor could yet resolve the doubt
Whether he should stay or go,
In those fields not far away
There was many a frolic swain,
In fresh russets day by day,
That kept revels on the plain.
Nimble Tom, surnamed the Tup,
For his pipe without a peer,
And could tickle Trenchmore up,
As 'twould joy your heart to hear.
Ralph as much renowned for skill,
That the tabor touched so well ;
For his gittern, little Gill,
That all other did excel.
Rock and Rollo every way,
Who still led the rustic ging,
And could troll a roundelay
That would make the fields to ring ;
Colin on his shalm so clear,
Many a high-pitched note that had,
And could make the echoes near
Shout as they were waxen mad.
Many a lusty swain beside,
That for nought but pleasure cared,
Having Dorilus espied,
And with him knew how it fared,
Thought from him they would remove
This strong melancholy fit,
Or so, should it not behove,
Quite to put him out of 's wit.
Having learnt a song, which he
Sometime to Sirena sent,
Full of jollity and glee,
When the nymph lived near to Trent,

They behind him softly got,
Lying on the earth along,
And when he suspected not,
Thus the jovial shepherds sung.

Near to the silver Trent,
  Sirena dwelleth:
She to whom Nature lent
  All that excelleth:
By which the Muses late,
  And the neat Graces,
Have for their greater state
  Taken their places:
Twisting an anadem,
  Wherewith to crown her,
As it belonged to them
  Most to renown her.
CHORUS.   On thy bank
  In a rank
  Let thy swans sing her,
And with their music
  Along let them bring her.

Tagus and Pactolus
  Are to thee debtor,
Nor for their gold to us
  Are they the better;
Henceforth of all the rest
  Be thou the river,
Which as the daintiest
  Puts them down ever,
For as my precious one
  O'er thee doth travel,

              She to pearl paragon
                Turneth thy gravel.
CHORUS.   On thy bank
                In a rank
                Let thy swans sing her,
              And with their music
                Along let them bring her.

              Our mournful Philomel,
                That rarest tuner,
              Henceforth in Aperil
                Shall wake the sooner,
              And to her shall complain
                From the thick cover,
              Redoubling every strain
                Over and over:
              For when my love too long
                Her chamber keepeth,
              As though it suffered wrong,
                The morning weepeth.
CHORUS.   On thy bank
                In a rank
                Let thy swans sing her,
              And with their music
                Along let them bring her.

              Oft have I seen the sun,
                To do her honour,
              Fix himself at his noon,
                To look upon her,
              And hath gilt every grove,
                Every hill near her,
              With his flames from above,
                Striving to cheer her;

And when she from his sight
    Hath herself turnéd,
He, as it had been night,
    In clouds hath mournéd:
CHORUS.   On thy bank
    In a rank
    Let thy swans sing her,
    And with their music
    Along let them bring her.

The verdant meads are seen,
    When she doth view them,
In fresh and gallant green
    Straight to renew them,
And every little grass
    Broad itself spreadeth,
Proud that this bonny lass
    Upon it treadeth:
Not flower is so sweet
    In this large cincture
But it upon her feet
    Leaveth some tincture.
CHORUS.   On thy bank
    In a rank
    Let thy swans sing her,
    And with their music
    Along let them bring her.

The fishes in the flood,
    When she doth angle,
For the hook strive a good
    Them to entangle;
And leaping on the land
    From the clear water,
Their scales upon the sand
    Lavishly scatter

   Therewith to pave the mould
    Whereon she passes,
   So herself to behold,
    As in her glasses.
CHORUS. On thy bank
    In a rank
     Let thy swans sing her,
    And with their music
     Along let them bring her.

   When she looks out by night,
    The stars stand gazing,
   Like comets to our sight
    Fearfully blazing,
   As wondering at her eyes
    With their much brightness,
   Which so amaze the skies,
    Dimming their lightness;
   The raging tempests are
    Calm when she speaketh,
   Such most delightsome balm
    From her lips breaketh.
CHORUS. On thy bank
    In a rank
     Let thy swans sing her,
    And with their music
     Along let them bring her.

   In all our Brittany
    There's not a fairer,
   Nor can you fit any,
    Should you compare her.
   Angels her eyelids keep,
    All hearts surprising,
   Which look whilst she doth sleep
    Like the sun's rising:

She alone of her kind
   Knoweth true measure,
And her unmatchéd mind
   Is Heaven's treasure :
CHORUS.   On thy bank
   In a rank
   Let thy swans sing her.
And with their music
   Along let them bring her.

Fair Dove and Darwin clear
   Boast ye your beauties,
To Trent, your mistress here,
   Yet pay your duties ;
My love was higher born
   Towards the full fountains,
Yet she doth Moorland scorn
   And the Peak mountains ;
Nor would she none should dream
   Where she abideth,
Humble as is the stream
   Which by her slideth.
CHORUS.   On thy bank
   In a rank
   Let thy swans sing her,
And with their music
   Along let them bring her.

Yet my poor rustic Muse
   Nothing can move her,
Nor the means I can use,
   Though her true lover :
Many a long winter's night
   Have I waked for her,

Yet this my piteous plight,
Nothing can stir her.
All thy sands, silver Trent,
Down to the Humber,
The sighs that I've spent
Never can number.
CHORUS.   On thy bank
In a rank
Let thy swans sing her,
And with their music
Along let them bring her.

Taken with this sudden song,
Least for mirth when he doth look,
His sad heart more deeply stung
Than the former care he took.
At their laughter and amazéd,
For a while he sat aghast,
But a little having gazéd,
Thus he them bespake at last:
"Is this time for mirth," quoth he,
"To a man with grief opprest?
Sinful wretches as you be,
May the sorrows in my breast
Light upon you one by one,
And as now you mock my woe,
When your mirth is turned to moan
May your like then serve you so."
When one swain among the rest
Thus him merrily bespake:
"Get thee up, thou arrant beast,
Fits this season love to make,
Take thy sheep-hook in thy hand,
Clap thy cur and set him on,

For our fields 'tis time to stand,
Or they quickly will be gone,
Roguish swineherds that repine
At our flocks, like beastly clowns,
Swear that they will bring their swine,
And will root up all our downs;
They their holly whips have braced,
And tough hazel goads have got;
Soundly they your sides will baste,
If their courage fail them not.
Of their purpose if they speed,
Then your bagpipes you may burn,
It is neither drone nor reed,
Shepherd, that will serve your turn :
Angry Olcon sets them on,
And against us part doth take
Ever since he was outgone,
Offering rhymes with us to make.
Yet if so our sheep-hooks hold,
Dearly shall our downs be bought,
For it never shall be told
We our sheep-walks sold for nought.
And we here have got us dogs,
Best of all the Western breed,
Which, though whelps, shall lug their hogs
Till they make their ears to bleed :
Therefore, shepherd, come away."
With this, Dorilus arose,
Whistles Cut-tail from his play,
And along with them he goes.

A FEW NOTES.

NOTE the not unfrequent use (especially in the "Barons' Wars") of *when* where we should now write *then*, in passing from one incident of a story to the next.

Also the use of *and* where we should now write *also;* the word *and* being in such cases placed where we should place the word *also*.

P. 23. *Lope-staves*, leaping-poles; *currers*, runners.

P. 39. *Morrians*, morions, helmets without visors, from Spanish, *morra*, the crown of the head.

Pouldron, or *pauldron*, a piece of armour covering the shoulder. Spanish, *espaldaron* from *espalda;* French, *épaule;* the shoulder.

Saltoir, *saltire*, in heraldry two bends forming a St. Andrew's cross, from *sautoir* a stirrup, which is from *sauter*, Latin *saltare*, to leap (on horseback).

Verry or *vair*, Old French for weasel-skin, a grey and white fur, from Latin *varius*, was used in heraldry for ground on a shield formed into a pattern with rows of silver and blue bells, arranged so that the spaces between blue bells form the silver bells inverted. Confusion between this word *vair* for fur and *verre* for glass, caused Cinderella's fur slipper in the French fairy story to become a glass slipper in English.

P. 45. *Segges*, sedges; *swound*, swoon; *prease*, press.

P. 65. *Guyne*, Guienne.

P. 89. *Corsives*, corrosives.

P. 147. *Cauples*, horses; Latin, *caballus*; Spanish, *caballo*; French, *cheval*.

P. 157. *Bet*, beat; *bourgonet* (French, *bourguignotte*), a form of helmet first used by the Burgundians. It was so fitted to the gorget that the head moved freely without producing a chink through which an enemy might pierce the neck.

P. 168. *Imp'd*, from old English *impen*, to graft. In days of hawking, sound feathers were fitted in the place of broken or bruised ones in the hawk's wing or tail to maintain power of flight.

So Shakespeare in Richard II., "Imp out our drooping country's broken wing." Imp also was used in gardening for a graft on a stock, and so applied to those who are now called scions (cuttings grafted) of a noble house. Thence children, thence mischievous little creatures, thence the imps of Satan.

P. 176. The *kerne* and Irish *galliglass*. *Kerne*, from Irish *cearn*, a man, was the light-armed Irish foot-soldier, as distinguished from the gallowglass (Irish *galloglach*) who was heavy-armed.

P. 249. Dive the *brack;* dip into the sea. Brack, the word from which we get brackish, used for briny, is often used by Drayton for the water of the sea; "scorned that the brack should kiss her following keel;" and when the chariots of the Egyptians are overturned in the Red Sea, Drayton makes them drag, as they float, the horses—

"Drag their fat carcase through the foamy brack
That drew it late undauntedly in pride."

In one place, Drayton applies the word to river water—

"Where in clear rivers beautified with flowers,
The silver Naïads bathe them in the brack."

P. 255. The *bi-cliff* hill. Two-peaked Parnassus.

P. 268. Like *sleave* was matted; sleave was floss silk, unspun, in knots or loops. Compare Shakespeare's "Sleep that knits up the ravelled sleave of care."

P. 273. *Dray*, an old word for a squirrel's nest, used as late as by Cowper, "Climbed like a squirrel to his dray."

www.ingramcontent.com/pod-product-compliance
Lightning Source LLC
Chambersburg PA
CBHW031342230426
43670CB00006B/412